AF268857

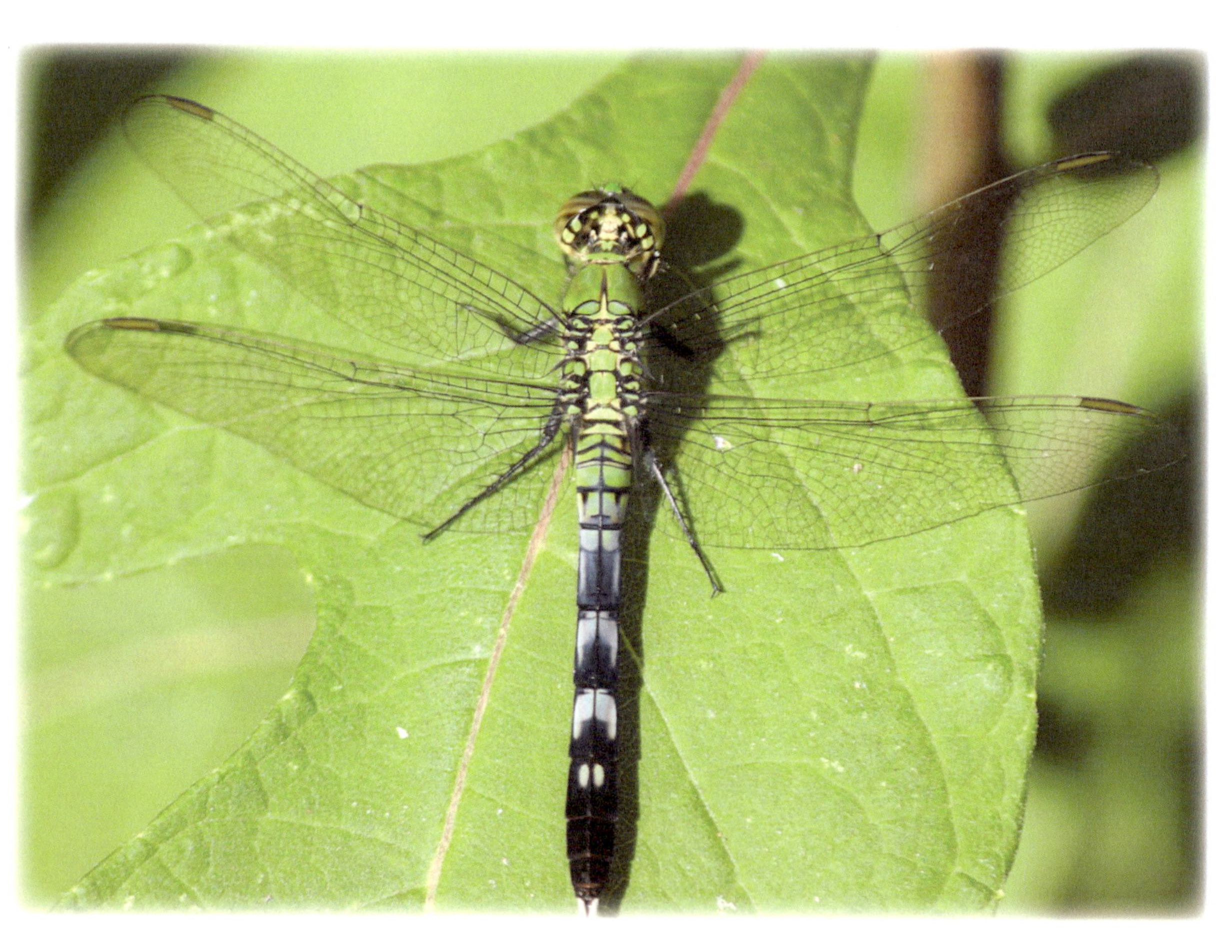

Reverie
Wing & Fin
Fur & Scale

Marian Blue
Poetry

Cherie Ude-Crowe
Photography

Sunbreak Press
Clinton, Washington

REVERIE *Wing & Fin Fur & Scale*

Copyright © 2023 Sunbreak Press

No part of this book may be used or reproduced in any manner whatsoever without the prior written permission of the publisher and copyright owner.
Cover Photo by Cherie Ude

Library of Congress Control Number: 2023945588

ISBN
Paperback 978-1-7321287-9-8
Hardback 978-1-7357093-0-7

Produced in the United States of America

First Edition
Published by Sunbreak Press
PO Box 145
Clinton, WA 98236
sunbreakpress.com

Acknowledgements

We wish to acknowledge the substantial help, advice, and support of the many family members, friends, and teachers who have made creating this book joyful. We individuals, like a book, are composites of experiences and influences from many individuals (animal, human, plant, and environmental). Comments on this work in particular have come from a variety of individuals.

Special thanks to Lois Edstrom who carefully read and wrote comments as a first reader. Not only is she an outstanding poet (see more about her work at http://loisedstrom.com), but also her ability to zero in on details (from sounds to coherence) and make clear and concise suggestions has helped improve individual poems and the book as a whole. She is an outstanding editor. We're very grateful she took time out of her busy life to help us out.

Thank you, too, to Malaika King Albrecht, for her generosity is taking time to write a blurb for this book. She's a very busy award-winning poet of four books, editor and founder of Redheaded Stepchild Magazine, and moderator of a weekly book launch for writers (https://www.youtube.com/user/malaika888/videos). She is also an award-winning visual artist who "prefers metal and fire to watercolors, aka the Metal Grandma" (https://www.facebook.com/Freckles-Farm-Metal-Works-100399398635979). In addition, Malaika is a yoga instructor, Reiki Practitioner, and HeartMath Certified Coach. Her volunteer work teaching therapeutic riding to those with disabilities has received national attention. She also is busy with her own farm. Learn more about her at https://sites.google.com/site/malaikakingalbrecht/.

Our gratitude includes those organizations that educate the public about our world, including those in which both Ude-Crowe and Blue have been able to participate: Sound Water Stewards (soundwaterstewards.org) (formerly BeachWatchers); Forest Stewardship University (https://forestry.wsu.edu/fsu/) and Forest Stewardship Program (https://www.dnr.wa.gov/publications/fp_sflo_fsp_brochure.pdf?llupt) through Washington State University extension and Forest Service Department of Agriculture. During Covid shutdowns, many online opportunities also became available, such as Your Daily Dose of Nature through Natural Habitat Adventures.

Thank you to Parks & Points (parksandpoints.com) for the work they do in celebrating the national world. The poem/picture for Viera Wetlands is from their Spring 2021 magazine.

Blue is especially grateful for Cherie Ude-Crowe's generosity in sharing her photographs, which capture the world in bountiful ways that manifest the magic in nature. Those photographs have always provided Blue with inspiration and enthusiasm. Ude-Crowe has made this work possible and joyful.

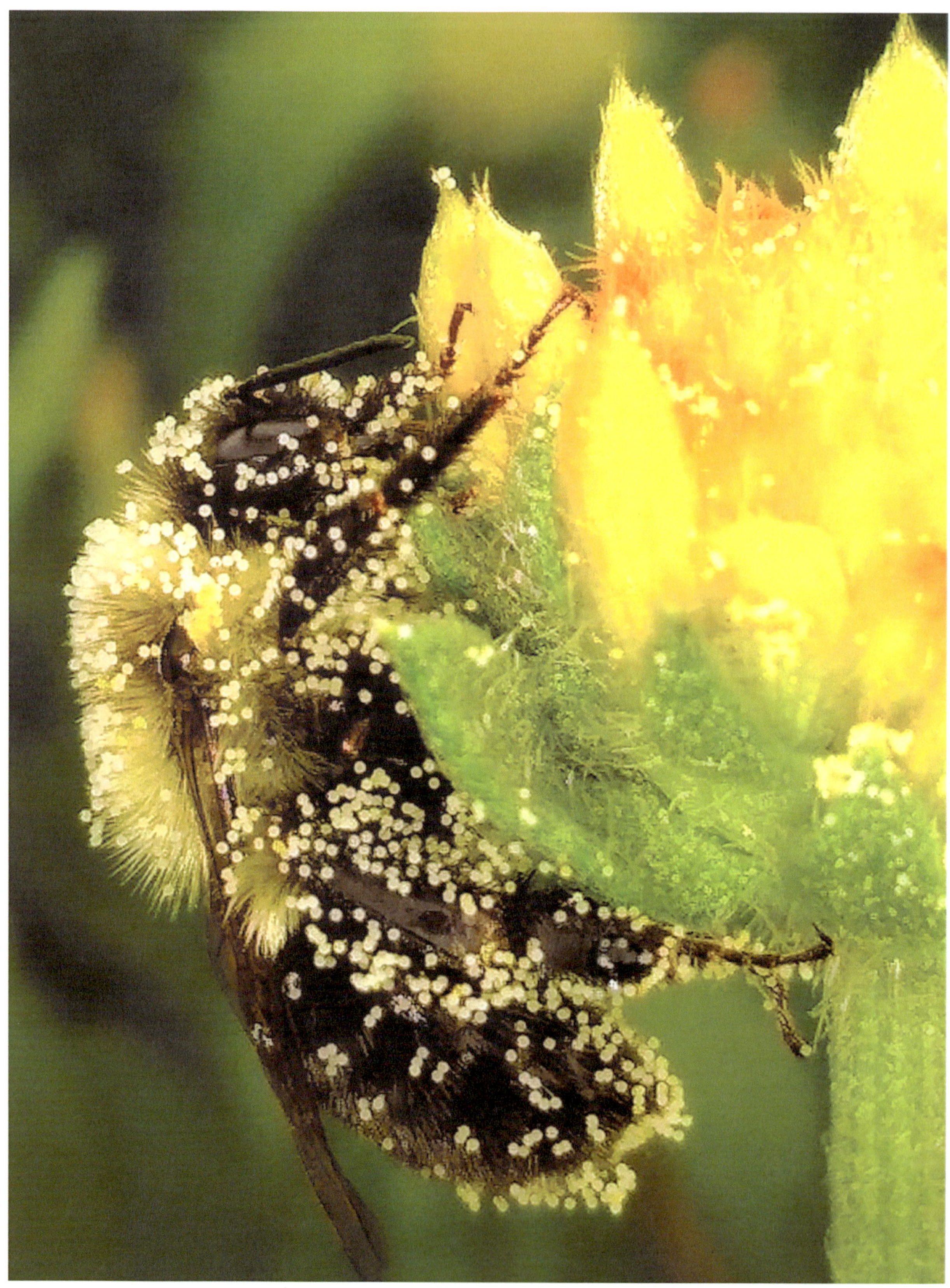

FOR EARTH

AND ALL HER PROGENY OF WING & FIN, FUR & SCALE

WITH GRATITUDE AND HOPE FOR A SAFE ENVIRONMENT

FOR GENERATIONS TO COME

Table of Contents

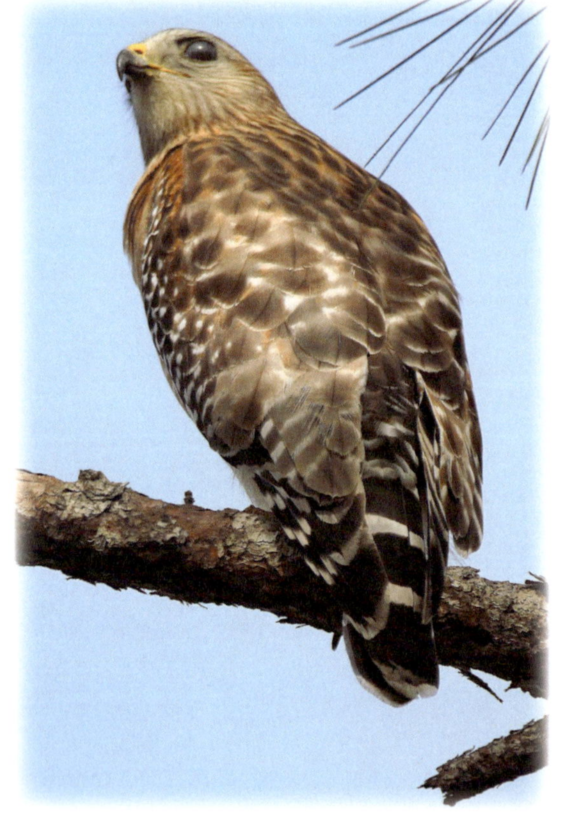

About the Authors
Other books by the Authors

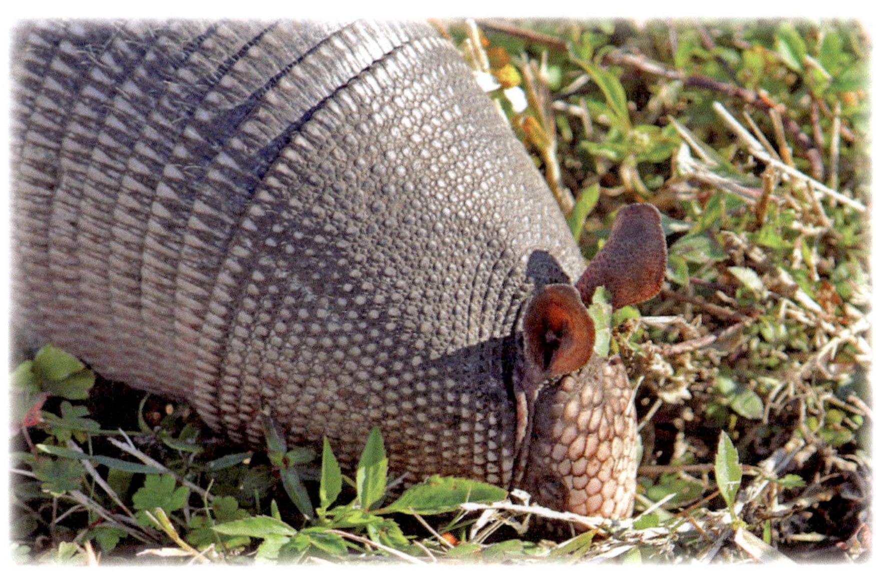

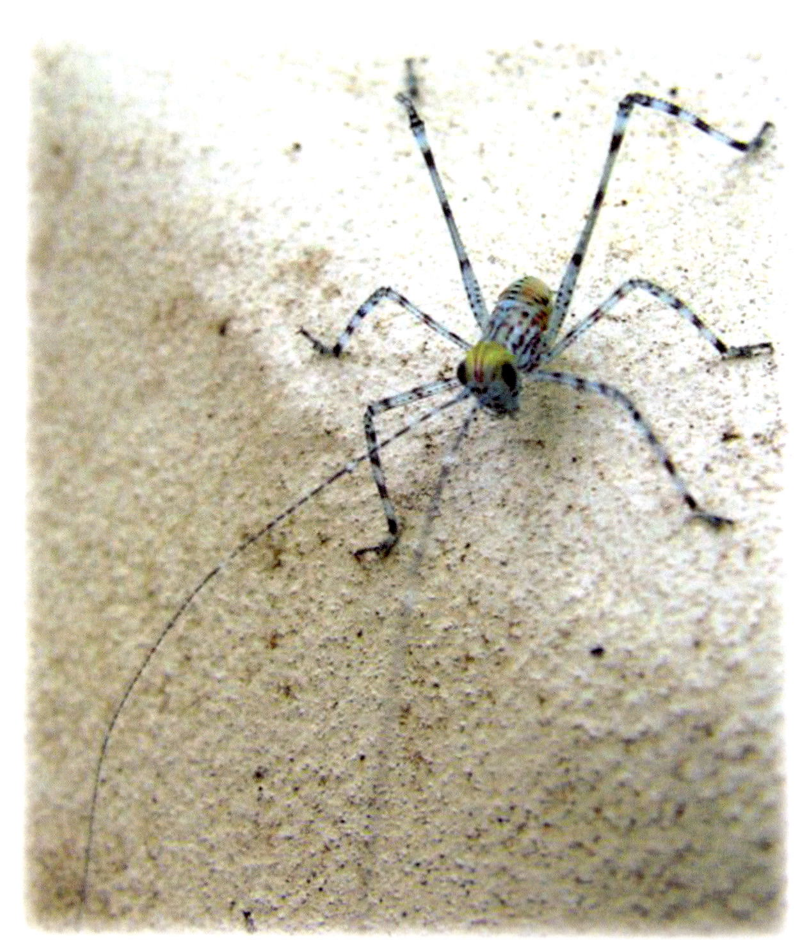

Forward

Blink.

That one-third of a second is gone.
Yet during that blink,
>   hundreds of whales breached
>   millions of birds lifted off Earth
>   clouds grew dark & storms formed
>   billions of other creatures blinked
>   a thousand gallons of water spilled over Niagara Falls
>   waves broke along more than 300,000 miles of shoreline
>   someone's grandmother died; someone's future grandmother was born
>   300 stars exploded, 15 thousand stars were born, 15 million rogue planets formed.

And how many times have you blinked while you read that?

Miracles ricochet around us in eyeblinks and light winks:
>   the mystical moment when thousands of bats all rise out of a cave at twilight;
>   the murmuring turn when hundreds of wingbeats and soft flight calls merge into
>   sky designs;
>   the moment of conception;
>   perfect harmony within music.

A wilderness of blinks. Unrepeatable. Unpredictable. Unstoppable. Unchangeable. Uncontrollable. And extremely easy to miss.

The trick is to notice your world during and between blinks. See the living and dying; feel the air cooling and heating; smell the suggestions of rain and wildflower blooms; hear frogs and birds and coyote songs; taste fear when the unexpected sparks adrenalin. This is magic, mystery, spirituality, joy, and infinite blessings rolled into daily life.

Blink.

Notice.

In these poems and photographs, we explore some of the humor, joy, beauty, and wonder we see, love and cherish. We're not scientists, but we hope that some of it will spark ideas for you, help awaken new awareness to your own magic. Don't miss one blinking moment.

Blink.

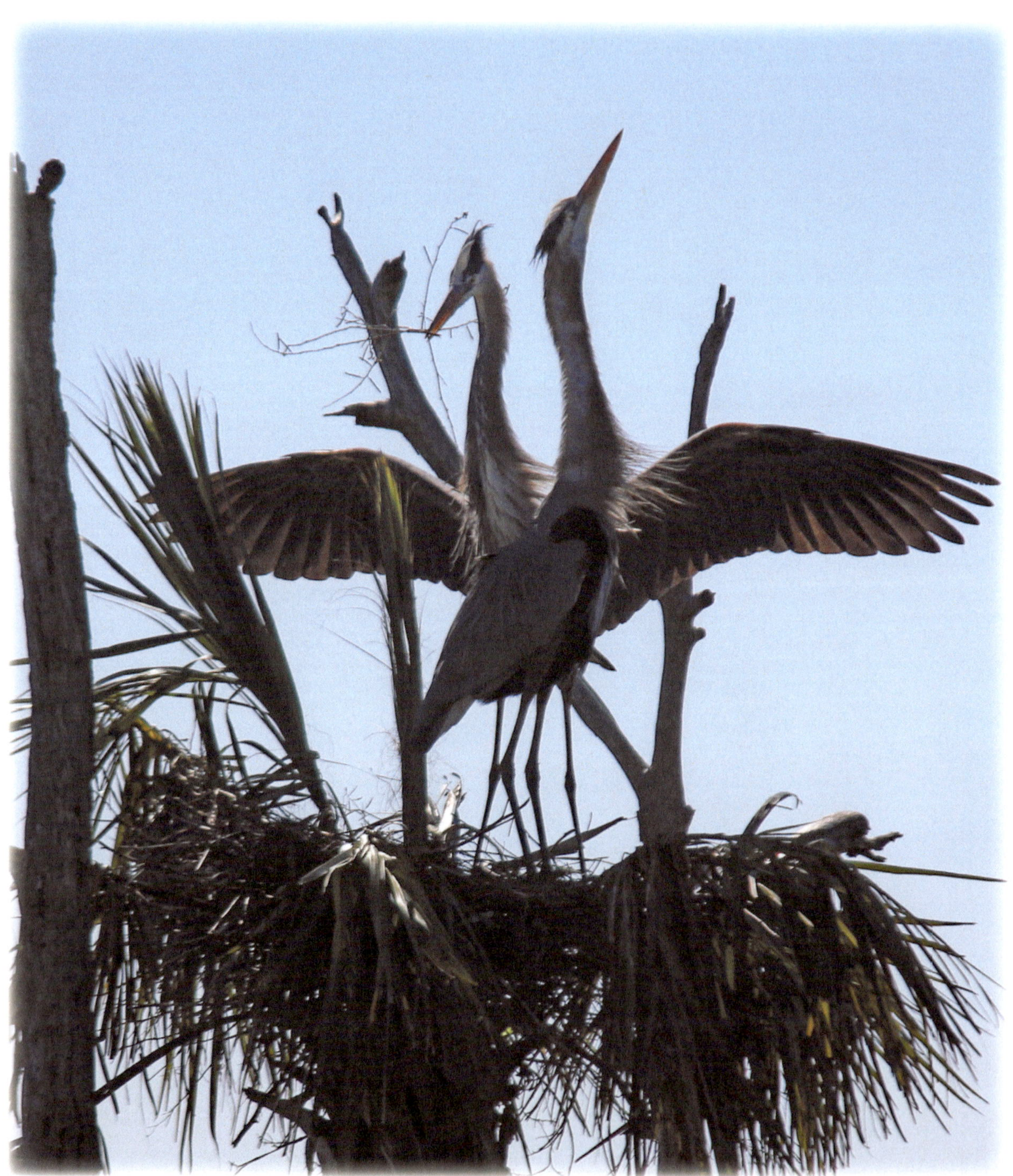

REVERY

To make a prairie it takes a clover
and one bee,
One clover, and a bee,
And revery.
The revery alone will do,
If bees are few.

--Emily Dickinson, 1896
Amherst College Digital Collections

ANECDOTAL SHINY THINGS

Crows pick up shiny things
– so I've been told –
like poets pick up images.
They flip them upside down,
and pull them inside out.
They toss them up to fall
through light, catching sparks,
firing imagination, burning
away routine, the hum-drum,
the patterned expectation.

Or so the stories go.
Scientists, less poetic than crows,
ignore the lure of shiny
things. They prefer empirical
data to support expectations.
Scientists extract the mundane
repetitive, predictable patterns,
leave the anecdotal stories
as informal logical fallacy.

Yet the crow at Rialto Beach
joined me, fixed me with an
anecdotal eye, took a quarter
I anecdotally offered,
flew away and stashed it
somewhere, then returned
for another quarter – eight
times. When my quarters
were scientifically gone

$$(N - N = 0)$$

I returned to the parking lot.
A crow landed in my pick-up
bed. I anecdotally chose
to believe it the same crow,
now wealthy but hungry, who
shared my lunch until it, too,
was scientifically gone and so
it logically flew away.
I remember, too, the anecdotal
fledgling crow found on a busy
road. With blue eyes and mouth
wide for endless meals, she
grew up anecdotally taking
every pen I tried to use,
shiny or not. She chased,
caught, then stood firm
on the dog's ball.
Years later, I anecdotally
find pens, coins, buttons
and mummified food,
like treasured caesuras,
within gaps in tree trunks,
bottles, stony beaches,
shelved books and mossy roofs.

Today, my parrot anecdotally
tried to remove the snaps
off my new jacket, creating
illogical holes. Outside,
anecdotal stellar jays
pilfer dog bones, carry
them to tree stump tops
and then scream anecdotes
at confused canines below.

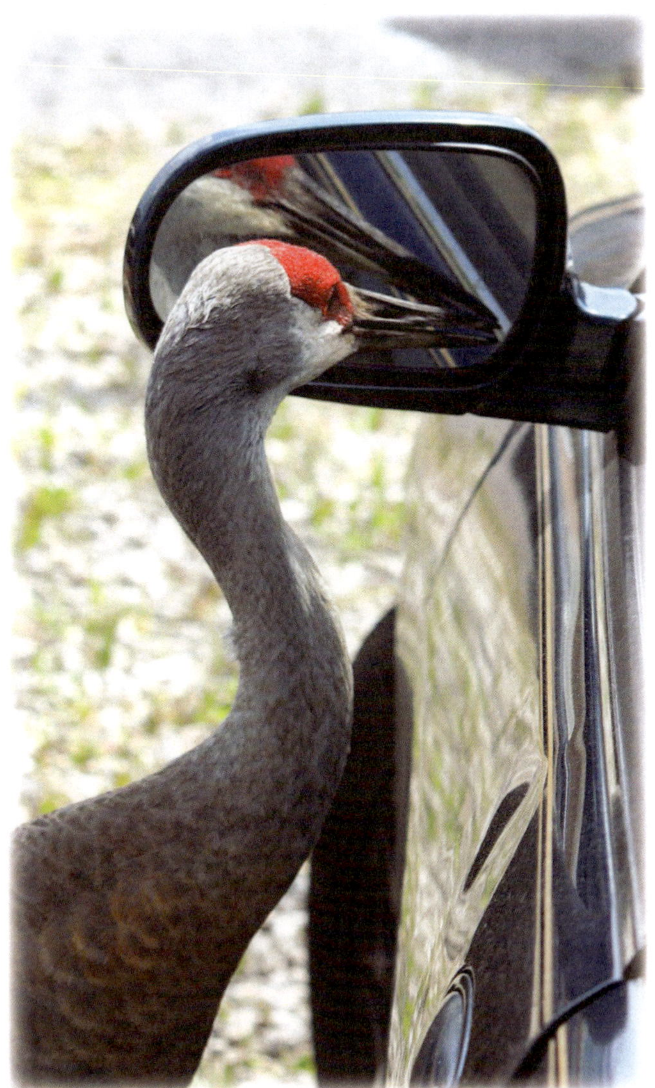

Not reliable, these anecdotal
pens and toys and food.
Empirical is dependable,
backed up with clever research,
brief and repeated experiments
with expectations of the same
outcomes, time after time,
as if birds and mammals,
—not humans, of course—
don't mind repeating the same
quarter games for the same
treats within the ruts of empirical
suburbia. Perhaps scientists,
unlike those they study
are immune to boredom. Perhaps
crows are anecdotally
more insightful than scientists
looking up at tree stump tops
and wondering why they're
teased by creatures who
don't know how to tease,
not in the empirical sense.

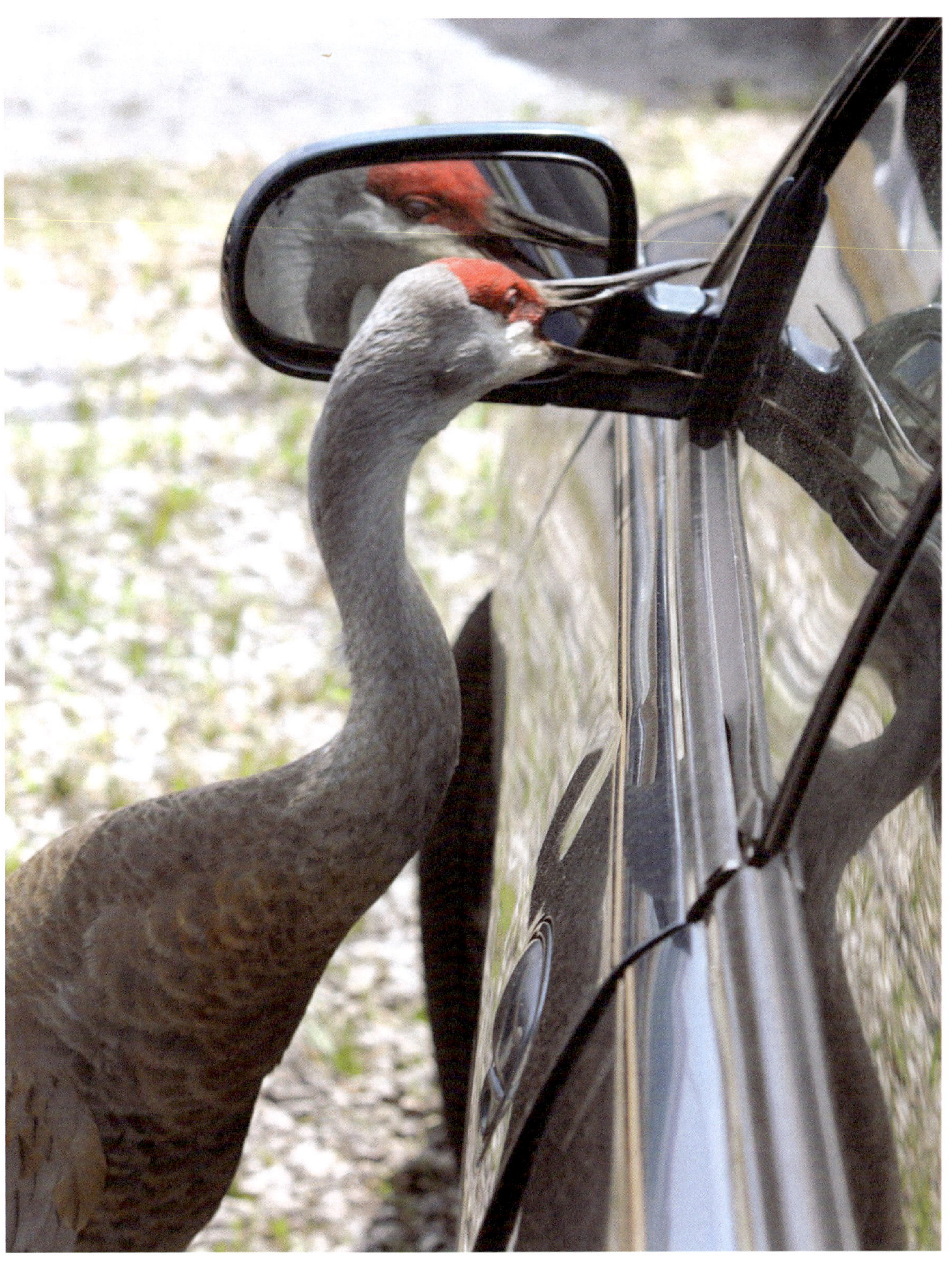

HOME AGAIN

The nest is vintage,
like grandmother's
moth-eaten wool coat.
Years have created
a home five feet wide
and four feet deep
but last winter's storms
carved a hole exposing
ground almost two-
hundred feet below.

Sticks, like a broken
jungle gym, poke out
at odd, jagged angles
slipping, sliding, and
falling when March wind
shakes the 8" thick limbs
of this three-hundred
year old Douglas fir,
broken, splintered top
fifteen feet above
the well-used nest.

He looks up, around
the misty blue sky
over open pastures
and a creek. Perfect
territory for finding
food for eaglets.
But the nest? ... perhaps
he's thinking he's
never seen it this bad.
Maybe a new nest?

But this one has proved
itself…not a chick
lost—ever. Supporting
branches are strong

and full. He again
looks around at green
expanse. Nothing else
as high, nothing else
with unlimited views.

 She hasn't arrived yet
for this eleventh
year. She might not want
to move, to start over.
Either way, it's one
stick at a time. He
flies off the large limb
overhanging the nest.

A week later, she
finally arrives. Did
she come earlier,
take a look and
decide to think
things over? Now she
perches on the limb
overlooking the nest.
He perches next to her,
watching, waiting. Then
she drops down into
the nest he's patched
and steadied and readied.
She starts rearranging,
testing the new weave,
ready for soft lining.

August, pierced by high-
pitched cries from above
where five eagles soar
in concentric circles.
Parents guide these young
in the hunt, the kill,
the search for thermals
high above the old
Douglas fir where their
nest sits secure above
everything in this
perfect territory.

Distant sounds—traffic,
children's squeals, dogs
barking, and chainsaws
growling—speak to other
lives being built and lived
where other trees stood.

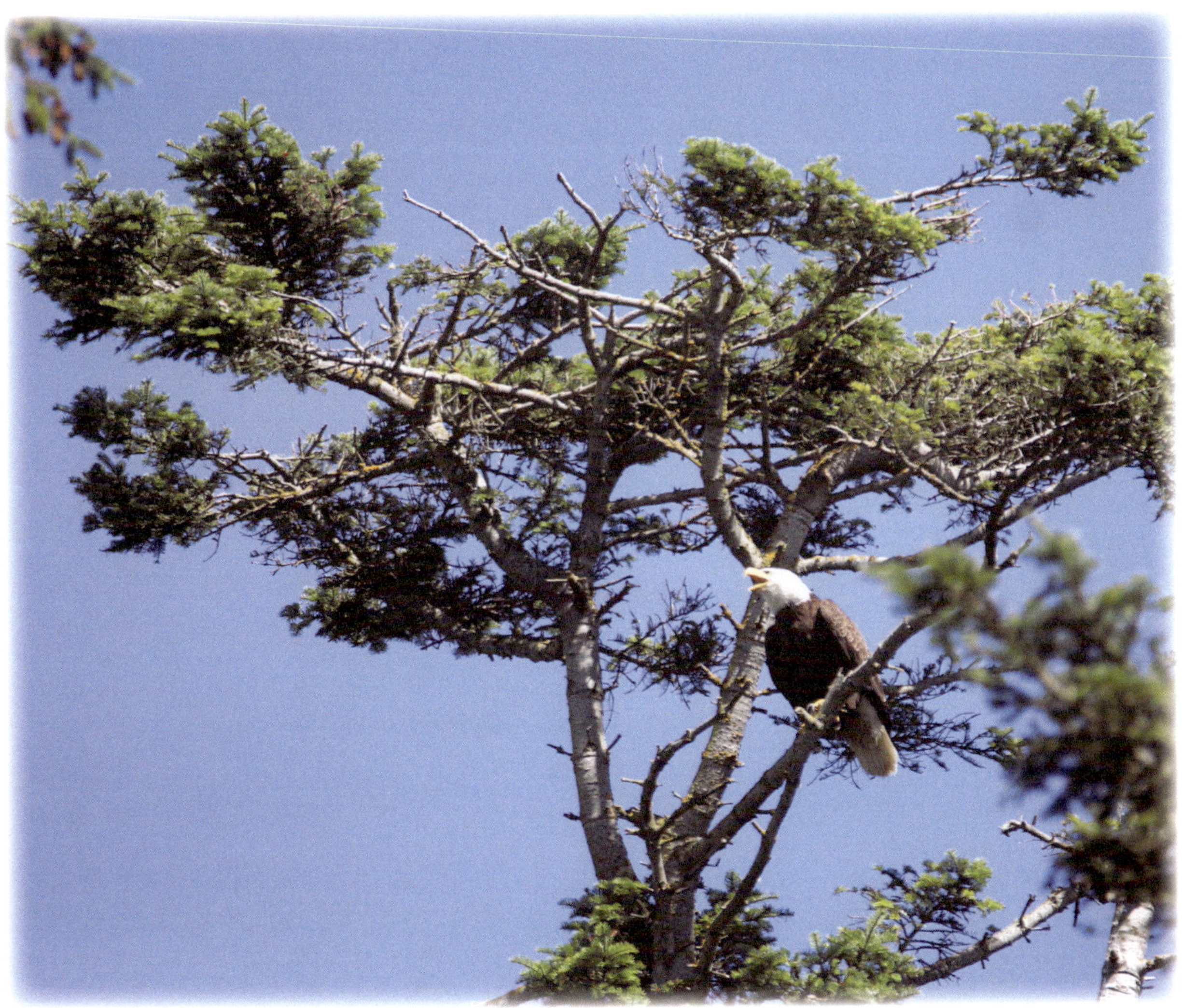

HARVEST

Doug squirrels scamper on
limbs 150' above, finding
ripe cones – sappy, slightly
green/brownish, and rock
hard – they throw–not drop.
These cones dent car hoods,
crash on metal roofs, frighten
birds and goats. Dogs break
into barks against intruders
they can't see or smell, only
hear like spirits in the night
that move coyotes to howl.

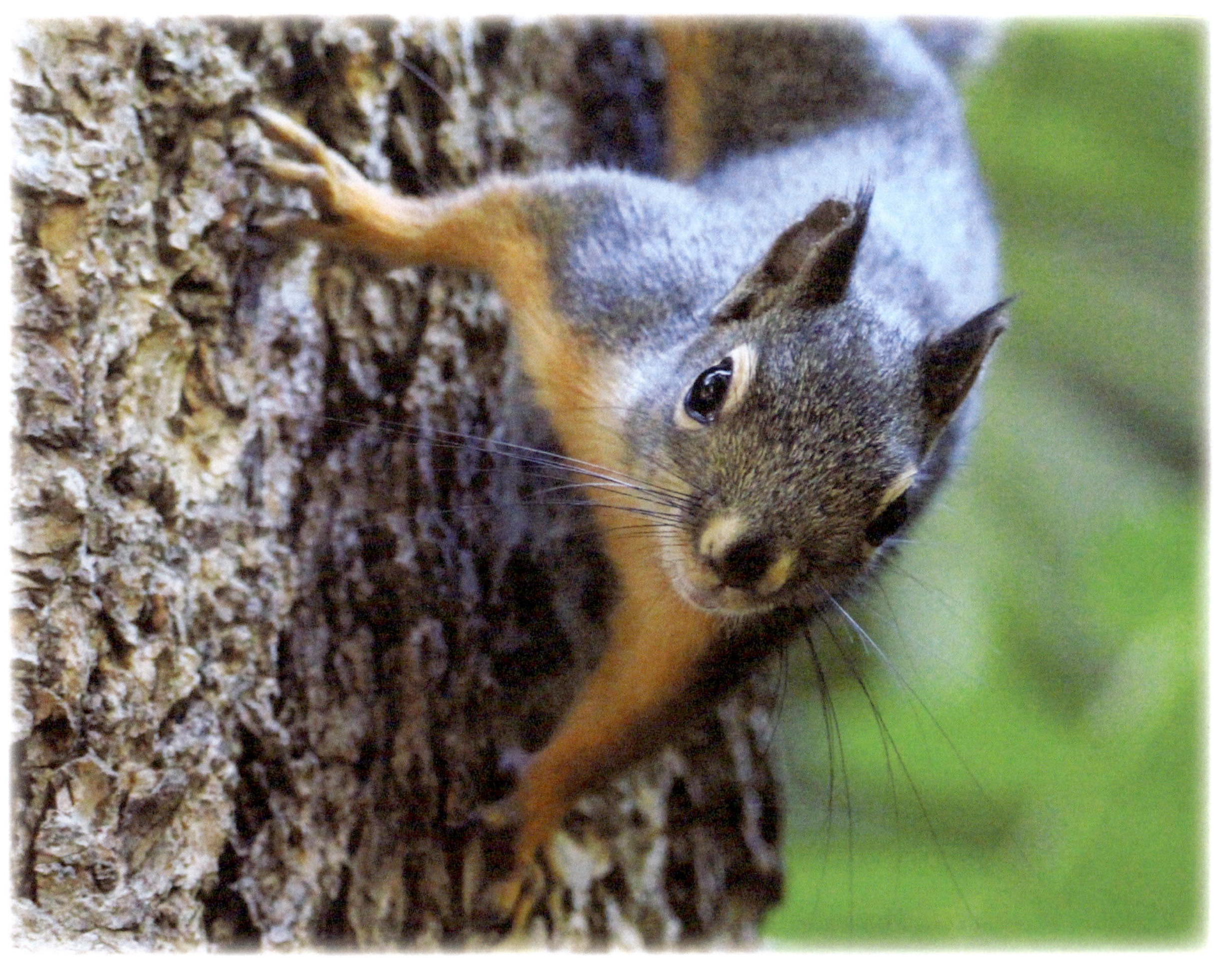

FEATHER HARVEST

Feather blizzards wrap us in down.

Fifty billion birds releasing thousands
of feathers each year–scattered below
trees, drifting lazily across schoolyards
and lawns, oceans and mountains, riding
breezes, exhaling memories of flight.

Why?

Feathers work hard, providing birds with
what they need for hunting and hiding;
waterproofing and warmth; sex appeal
when breeding. Yet, sun and wind, rain
and brush, age, and nest-sitting tatter
feathers' edges. Barbules and hooklets
wear away. Vanes fade and lose shape.
Simple preening and oiling no longer do.
Molt is a must and old feathers must fly.
Some lose a feather here or there;
seeing a difference requires a good eye.
But pity the poor penguins with molts
catastrophic, keeping them naked
and hungry, shore-bound for months.

Where Do they Go?

Trillions of feathers over millions
of years shed like Job's tears to sprout
anew. What if filoplume feathers
create seafoam; down makes up clouds
and trees sprout bristle feathers for leaves
waiting for Fall winds to renew their flight.
Feasibly, ferns are flight feathers who learned
how to grow. And those flower petals
must be contour feathers, colored for fun.

From flowers come seeds again taking
flight like the dandelion cypsela
who unfurls parachute-like pappus
for migration, maybe for miles before gently
settling, like comforters, on sleeping ground.

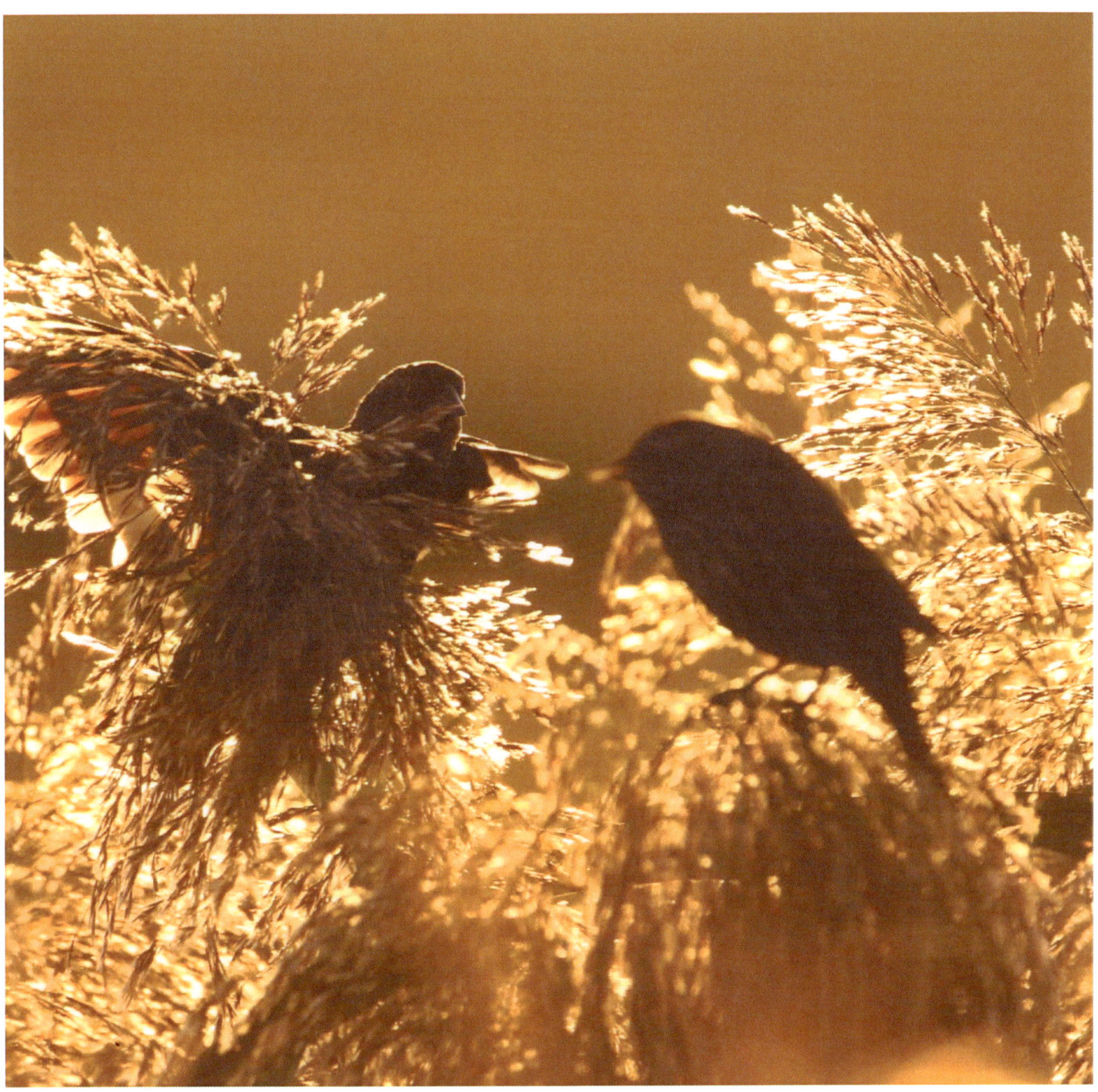

DIVERSITY OF UNDERSTANDING

Not all feet are equal,
most certainly not
the same. Feet specialize,
tell stories,
and complain.

What birds do
and how they do it
and where they live as well
are told in toes and claws
and soles like footnotes
on a page.

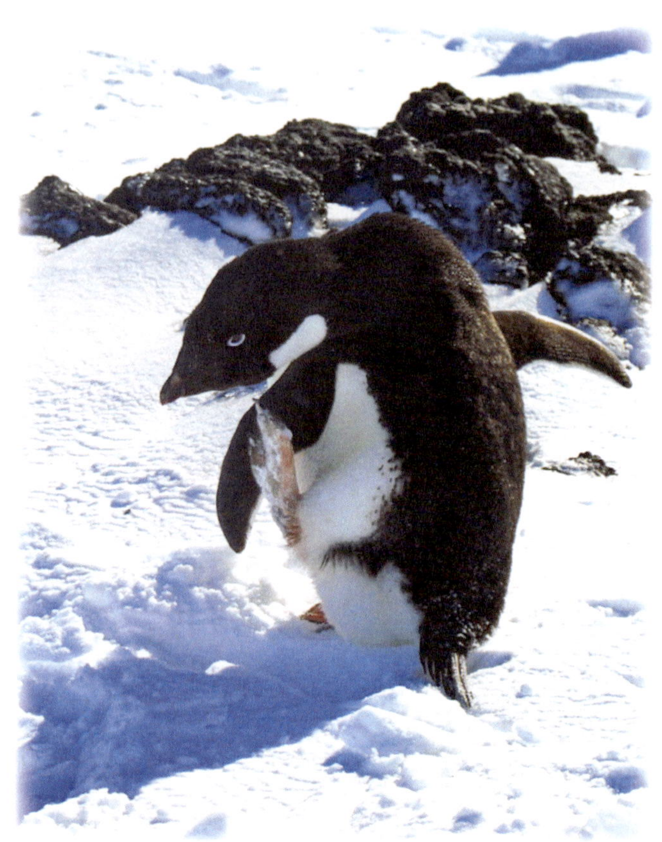

Ducks waddle and paddle
on broad, webbed feet*
perfect for swimming—
they've got a great glide—
but with legs set rearward,
they wobble on land
when others might stride.

Passeriformes perch,
three toes forward,
one behind, a secure
perching position,
one of the best
you'll find.
Chickadees to ravens
balance on wires, fences
and branches with bare
feet and legs
snugly warm…**
a simple squat
comforts them
in down.

With long necks, legs,
and arachnodactyly-
designed toes,
wading birds pose
along watery shores,
tutu-like feathers
fluffy and dry.
Those lengthy,
thin toes,
make mud-walking
and standing easy
to do, even
with a pause or two
for scratching
around to find
food of the bottom-
dwelling kind.

The zygodactyl design
is for those who climb:
two toes forward,
two toes behind.***
Owls and woodpeckers
share this trait
as do parrots
who use these flexible
feet to lift food
and hold it steady
to eat. The roadrunner
finds this design ideal
for desert speeding…
beep-beep.

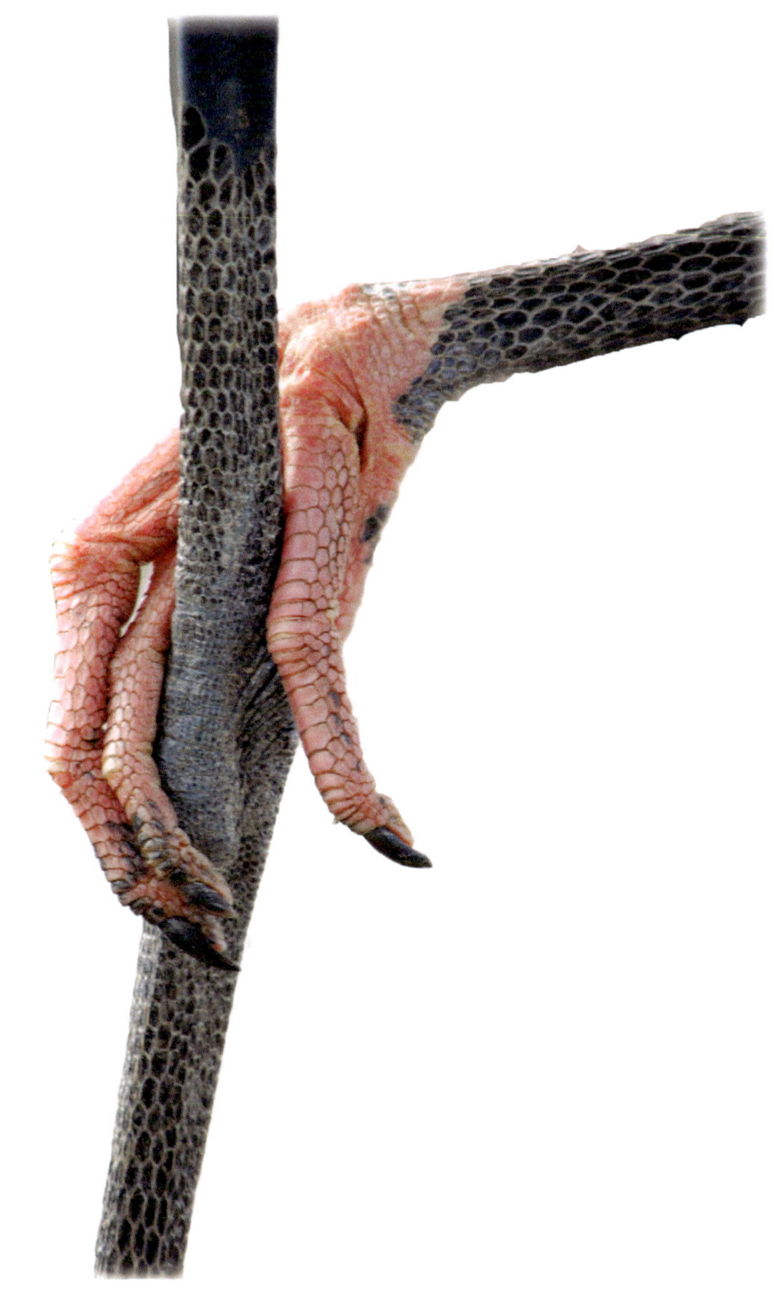

One bird has neither
four toes nor three.
An ostrich stands
on just two:
one large and one not.
The system works
fine for this huge bird
who lives without flight,
just running and kicking
and hanging out.

Birds are diverse,
and their stories are vast.
Many of these you'll
discover are told
within those toes
and claws
and soles.

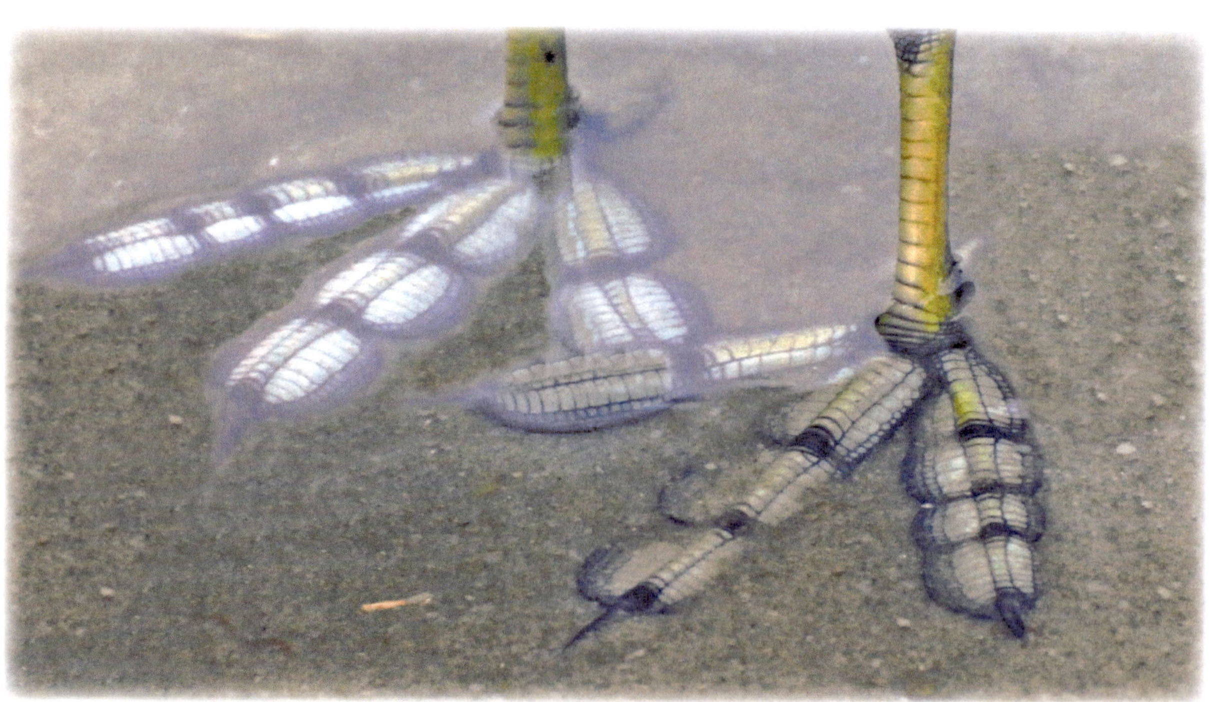

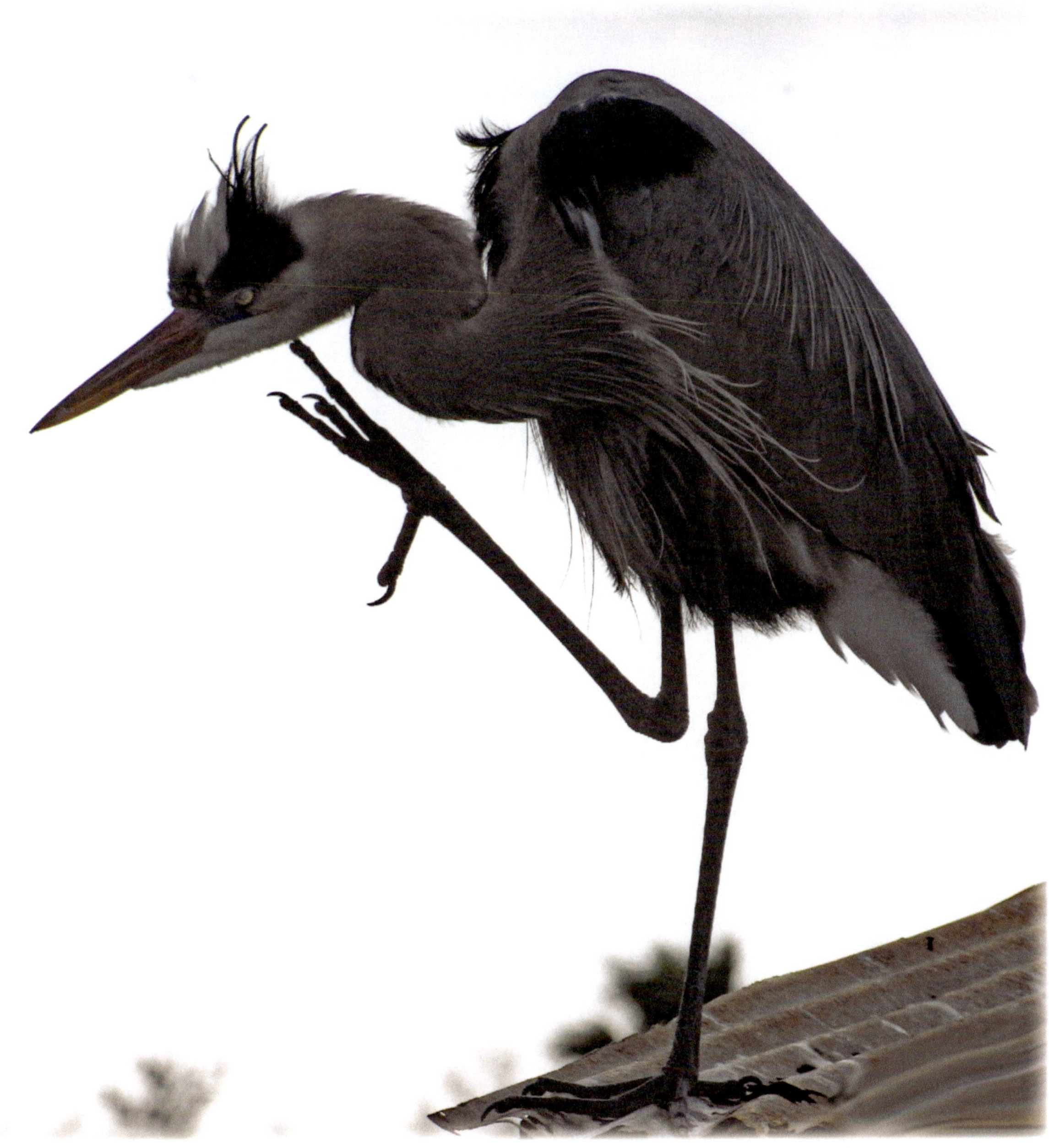

*They use a "smart" system, no Internet required, to provide a countercurrent heat exchange.
**Low fluid in feet cells combine with a talent: stand one leg at a time, keeping the other tucked in feathery warm.
***In wise design, backward toes can rotate for a sidewise grip on their tree trunk of choice.

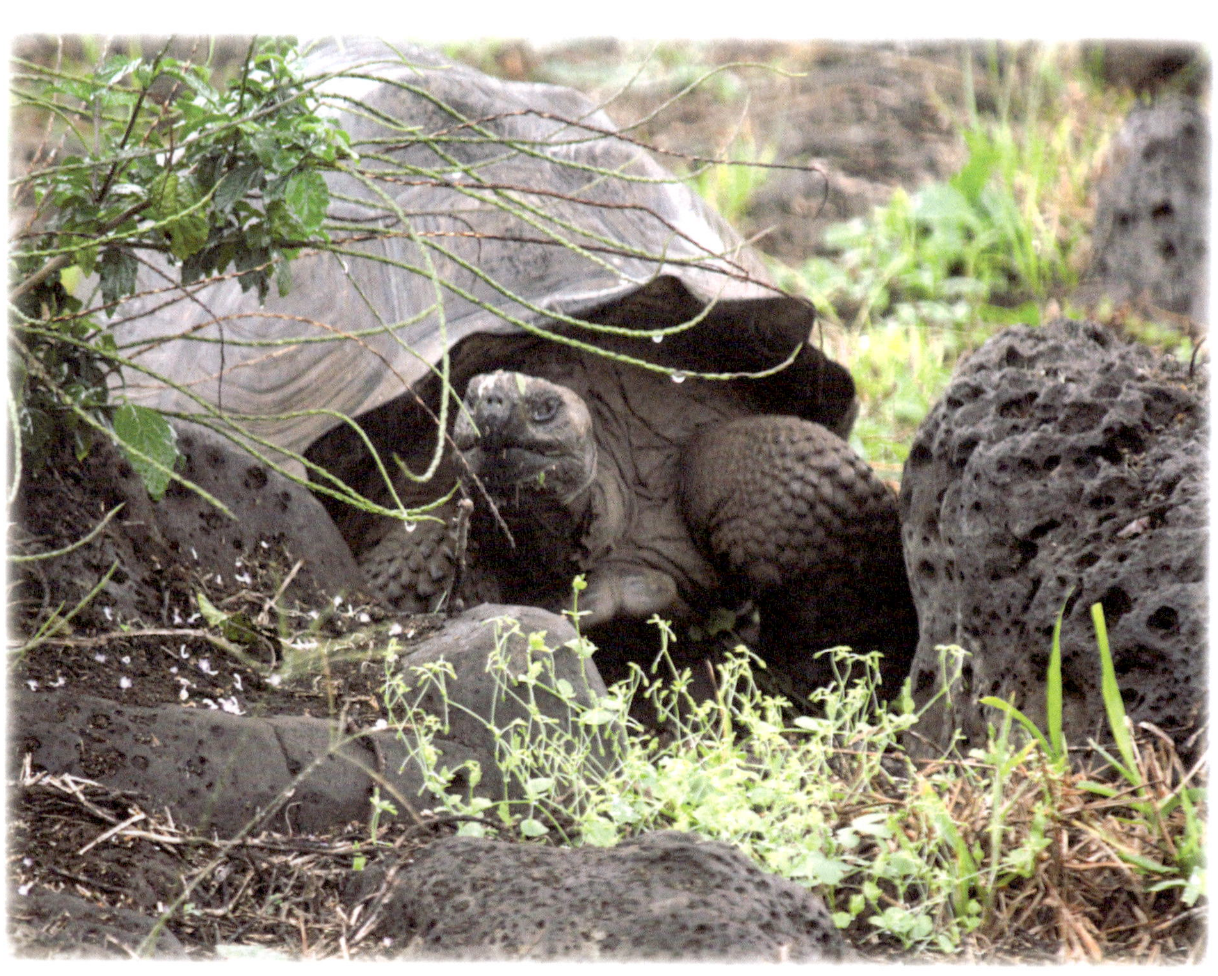

PAYING ATTENTION

"There is a way that nature speaks, that land speaks. Most of the time we are simply not patient enough, quiet enough, to pay attention to the story."

–Linda Hogan

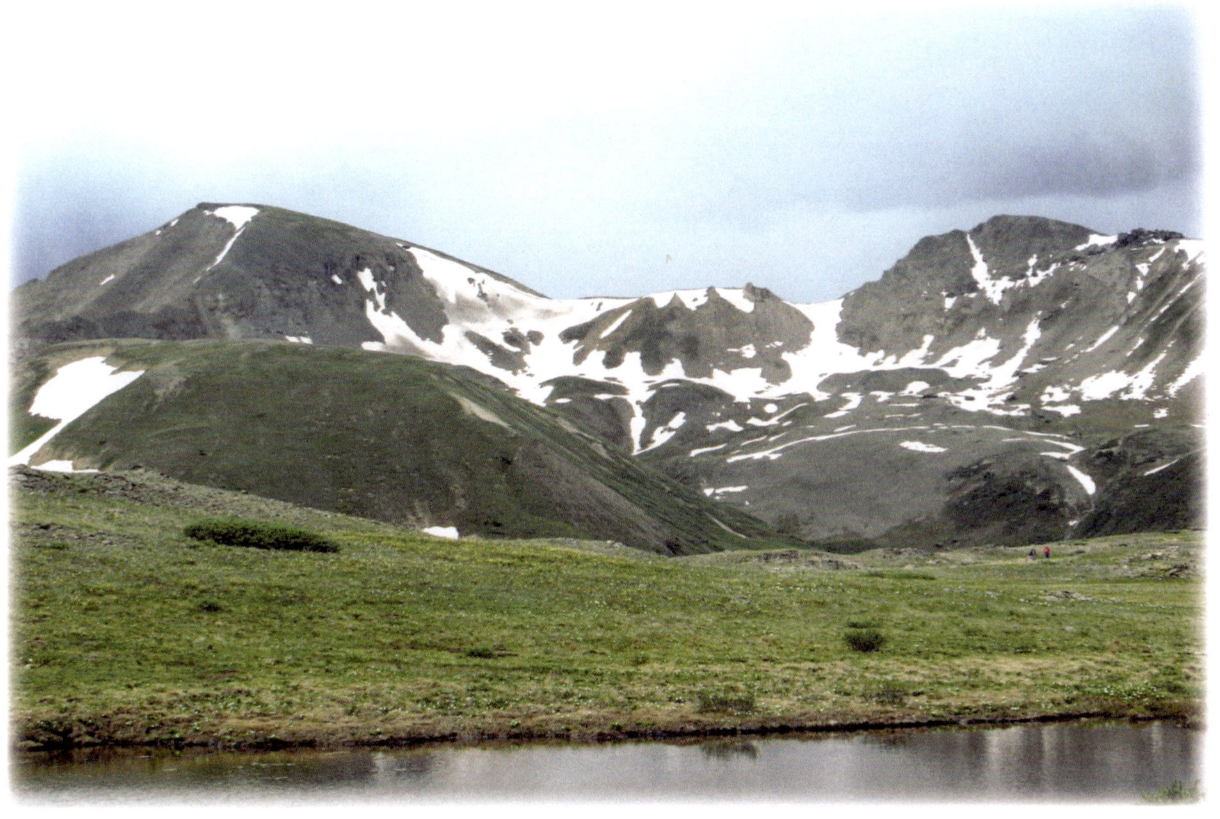

DRUMMING

> The earth has music for those who listen.
> —William Shakespeare

You've heard them, perhaps cursed them
    in spring
    at dawn
when the staccato beat raps and tats
on the metal gutter.

Drummers hammer tempos, rhythms
and styles that fit their particular clan.
Red-headed woodpeckers excel
at a one-billed but two-part rhythm
with occasional staccato beats. The tiny
downy perfects periodic one-second bursts,
19-25 beats per second, ostinato*. Yet,
each one ranges from traditional pockets,
uses a fill, a kick, a stylistic trick or two
tattooing out a personal song, pitch and woo.

The tap and drum flips, the musical changeup
in pitch, tone, and resonating thumps: low mutes
in snow and resounding hammers in dry,
blasting high volume on dead and hollow
trees, logs, and stumps, but best of all that metal
gutter, an echo chamber to wake a forest.
Of course, in a bind, any drummer has found
substitutes: trash can lids to frozen ground.**

Some early human no doubt heard this forest
beat, picked up a stick and joined the local elite,
rich with music, the beat of the seasons,
the territorial rhythm that must be heard.

Duke Ellington claimed a drum was a woman,
but woodpeckers, flickers, and sapsuckers know
the drum and drummer are one ... and it's a bird.

    * ostinato – a repeating pattern (drummed by multiple woodpeckers in this case)
    ** Palm cockatoos shake seed pods against hollow wood, cordon-bleus use their feet

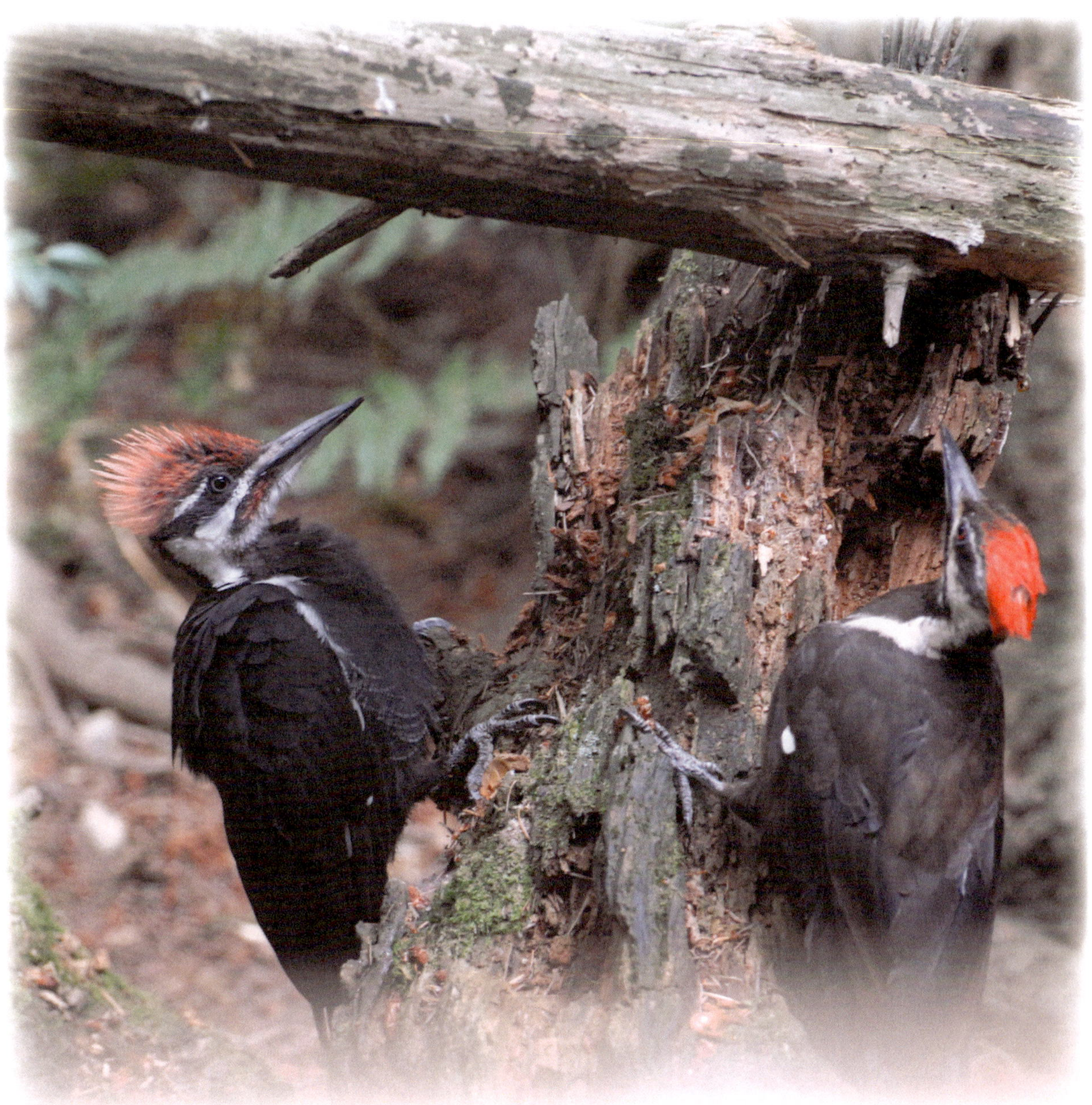

GREBE AND MOORHEN

One watches and one trusts,
thrusting an unseeing butt
and greenish legs up while
dining on a small fish,
a tadpole or even an
insect easily accessible to this
omnivorous, orange-billed
moorhen—aka swamp chicken—
maybe male, maybe female
since, like the ladybug, *hen*
possesses a liberal definition.

The grebe is, perchance, on watch
for this Moorhen, this other bird
with intriguing toes, not globed
like the grebe's, but still greenish
and long for tromping across
wetlands, and, therefore, a neighbor
even if not a friend. Or this grebe
might be just passing by, not now
interested in thrusting up toes,
beautiful and therefore valuable;
perhaps this grebe trusts less, not
quite as sure as the moorhen
that someone will sound the alarm,
spring into action, should a gator
or eagle come by for lunch. After
all, how trustworthy is a neighbor
who doesn't ask before taking a dive?

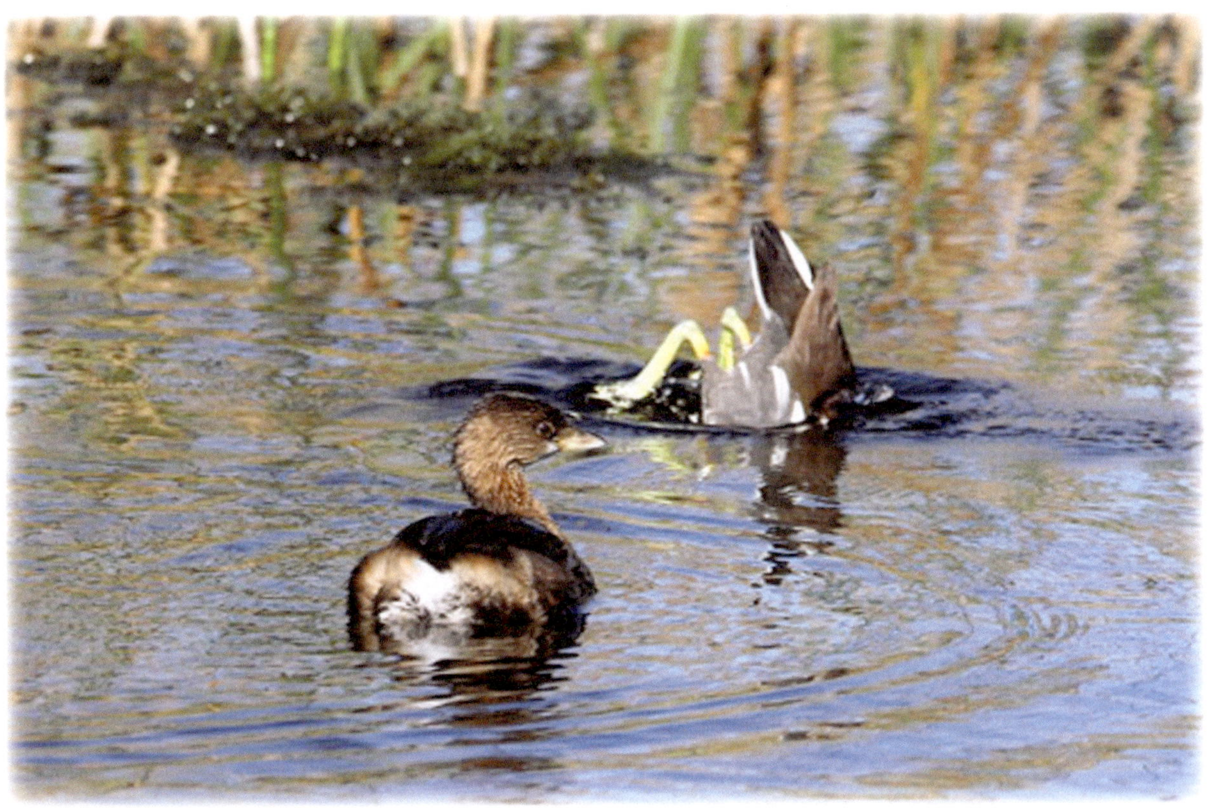

Coot

Look at that coot strutting down that bank,
head like a duck with a sharp white beak,
body like a chicken with legs quite long
and golly gosh darn! look at those feet!

With long-lobed toes like sweetgum leaves,
but the lobes fold back when the foot comes up
so the coot doesn't waddle, just scoots along.
Out for a swim, lobes web-wide, just watch those

coots bob and glide! Good as a duck is how
they swim. See that eye, blinking bright red!
Then pointy tail up and slurp goes a plant.
Living life fine, that's the mudhen coot.

They've got it all—except that voice! Squawk!
and Croak! and Squeak! and Grunt! Cousin
rails click, chuckle and trill but they can't swim
and feet are dull – stick-like toes sport no web.

And look at those coot chicks, baldly red-headed,
with their precocial* launch in a cool coot strut:
They've got it made—there's no compare
to the coot's flamboyant, birdie flair.

*Precocial: hatched with the ability to feed itself almost immediately.

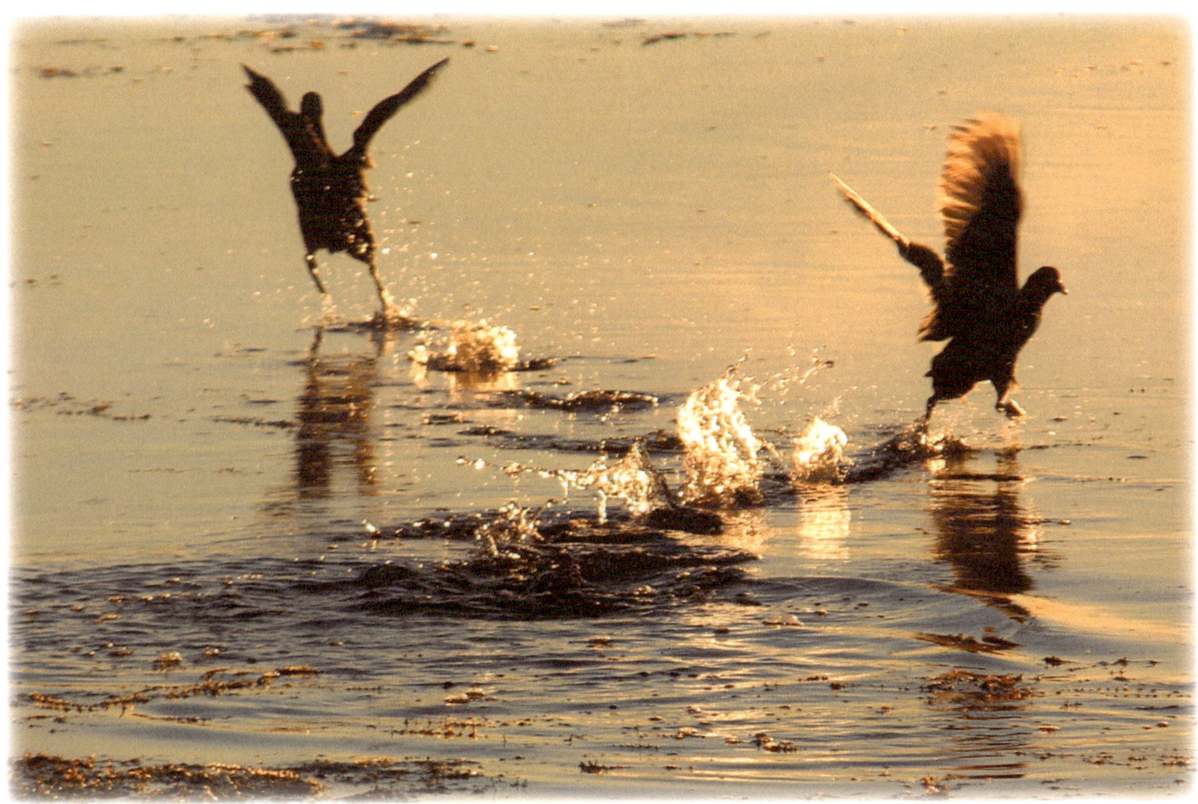

                    Marian Blue and Cherie Ude-Crowe

FIRST SPRING

They choreograph young,
step quickly
aware that to meditate
may eliminate the ability
to ambulate evermore.

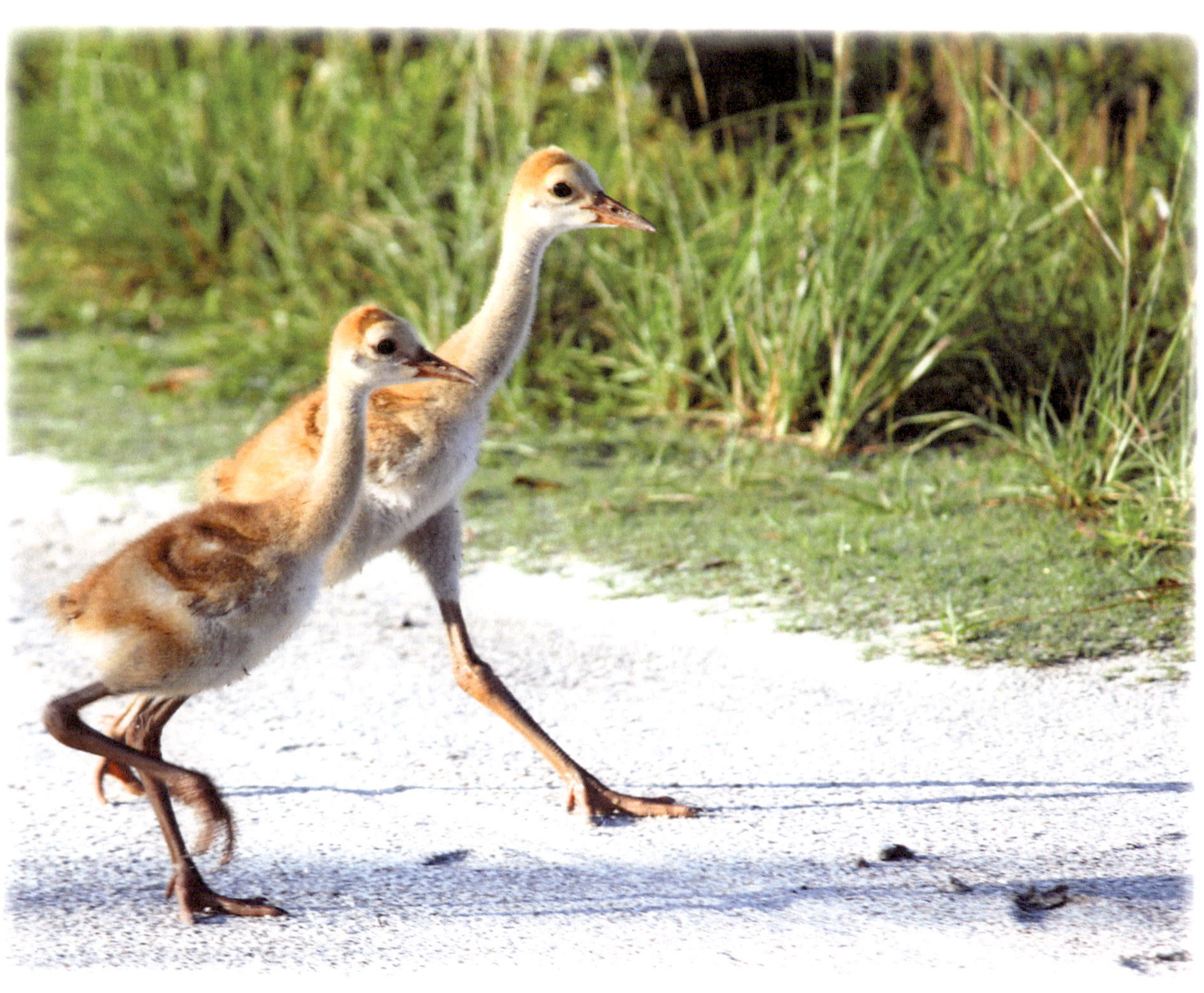

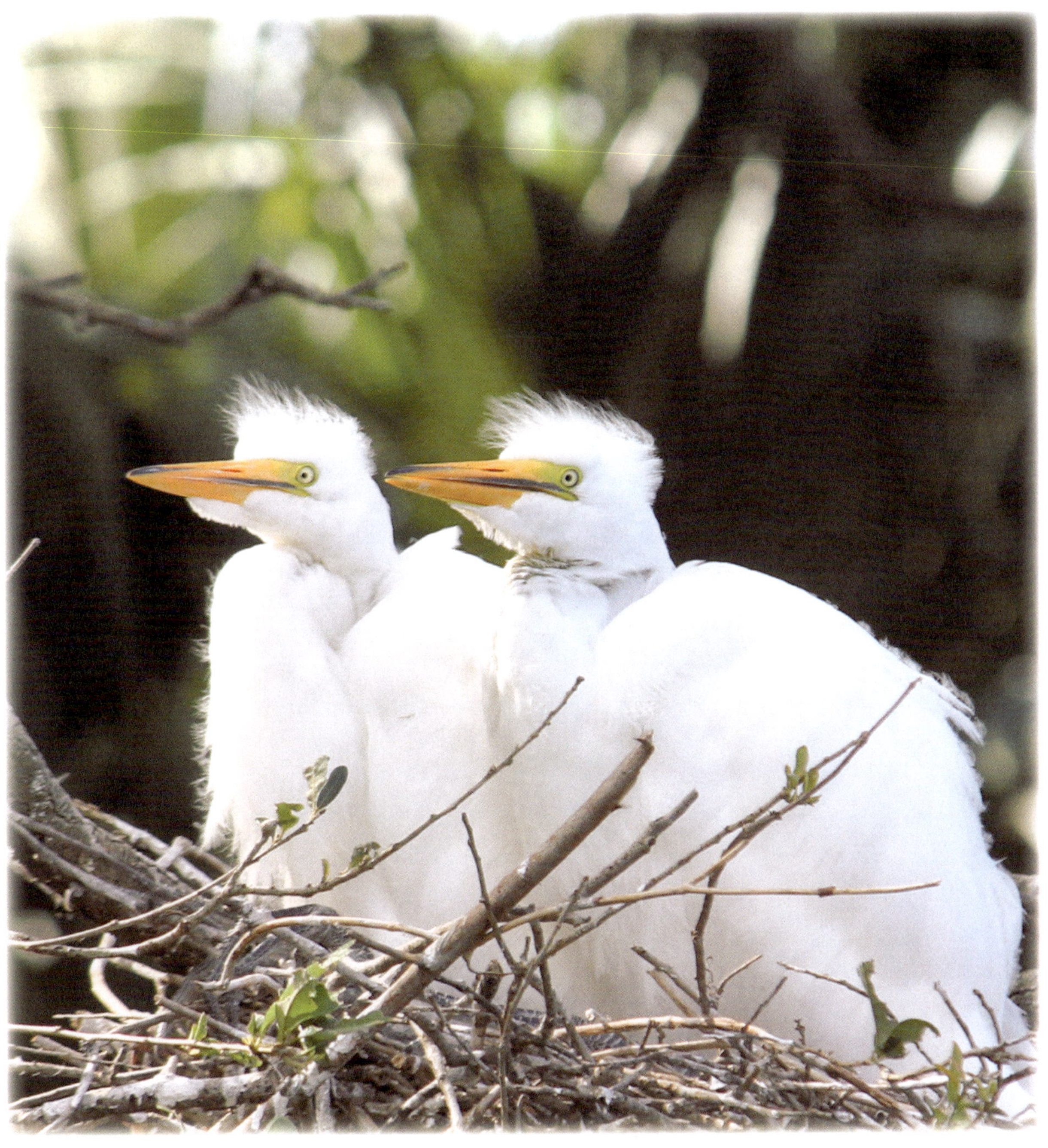

SKIMMER SKIMMING

A bird of legend and folklore,*
Skimmer plows a mirrored sky,
long lower mandible leaving
a wake rippling slowly away,
wrinkling water-bound cumulous
towers into cotton candy puffs,
dwindling pink in nautical twilight.

Skimmer furrows crisscross,
curving quests of aerial twists
and turns until beak and fish
connect. Bill snaps shut, neck
bends, then head whips up,
fish trapped. Skimmer soars
into sky sea pricked by stars.

They look like "…aerial beagles
hot on the scent of aerial rabbits."**

Do Skimmers ever worry about
rocks, boards, or – in tropical
climes – gators? Do they feel
brave or wonder if evolution
or revolution could find a better
way? Is there a choice?

Hatched with upper and lower
bill matching, what must it feel
like to have the lower bill grow
longer and longer still? Does
the head grow heavy and weary?
Yet youngsters not only learn
to make a living flying, at top
speed, they do so with that long,
lower bill plowing for dinner.

Skimmer spends no extra time
on nest design or hidden roost.
Skimmer has no long commute.
Nests are scraped out on sand
and when exhaustion strikes,
Skimmer flops down as though
tossed away by a careless hand.
Skimmer relies on the respect
of strolling strangers and pets,
to not disturb nests nor rest.

For now, Skimmer gulps, circles,
again meets Skimmer-self flying
upside down to dip and plow sky-
like water of fire, dark and light***.

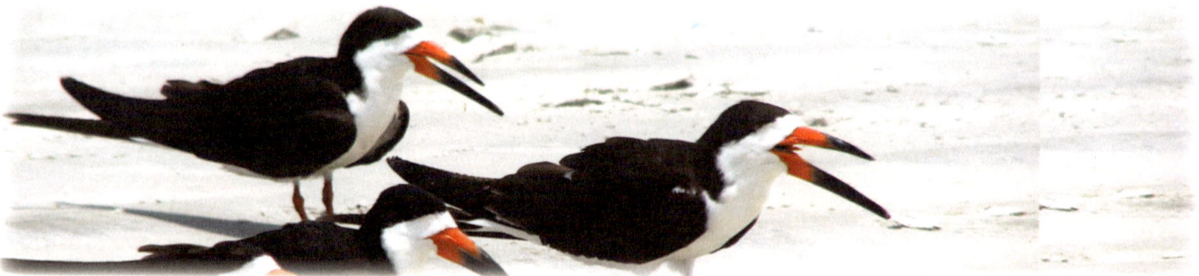

* The distinctive Black Skimmer has many folk names in North America, where it has been called scissor-bill, shear-water, seadog, flood gull, stormgull, razorbill, and cutwater.
**Quote of biologist R. C. Murphy in 1936
***Although the Black Skimmer is active throughout the day, it is largely crepuscular (active in the dawn and dusk) and even nocturnal. Its use of touch to catch fish lets it be successful in low light or darkness.

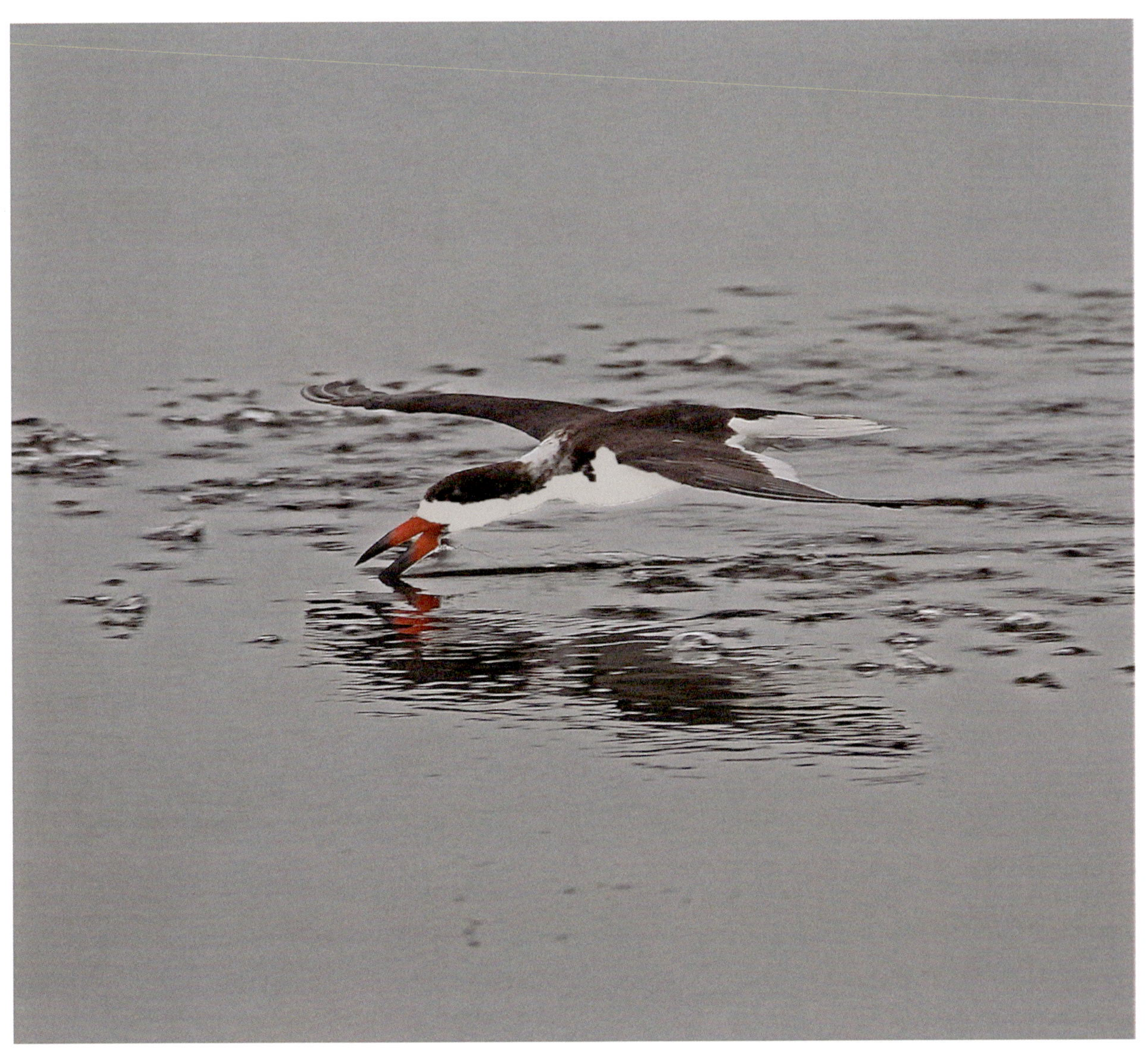

Sticky Situation for Egrets

Reedy, weedy, bushy wetlands—
abundant organic debris littering
each square inch within vast square
miles to equal incalculable quantities
of sticks
       the wrong diameter,
       the wrong length,
       the wrong flexibility
to please the fluffy-feathered mate
above, who snatches and then tosses
her partner's meticulous stick selection
out, to fall to reedy, weedy, bushy
wetlands below where another
harried mate studies the reject,
then carries it to his own fluffy-
feathered mate in their nest.

Success! She grabs and jabs the stick
into the edge of her pile of jumbled
branches. She pokes, shoves and weaves
it through the intricate mess, pulls
a different stick crosswise, jams it
against the new addition so four stick
ends poke out in different directions.

Somehow the woven pile of sticks,
carefully and illogically chosen,
endures wind, rain, hail, and a clutch
of chicks huddling mid-nest within
downy moss and feathers, endlessly
tidied every day by each and every
fussy and fluffy-feathered parent.

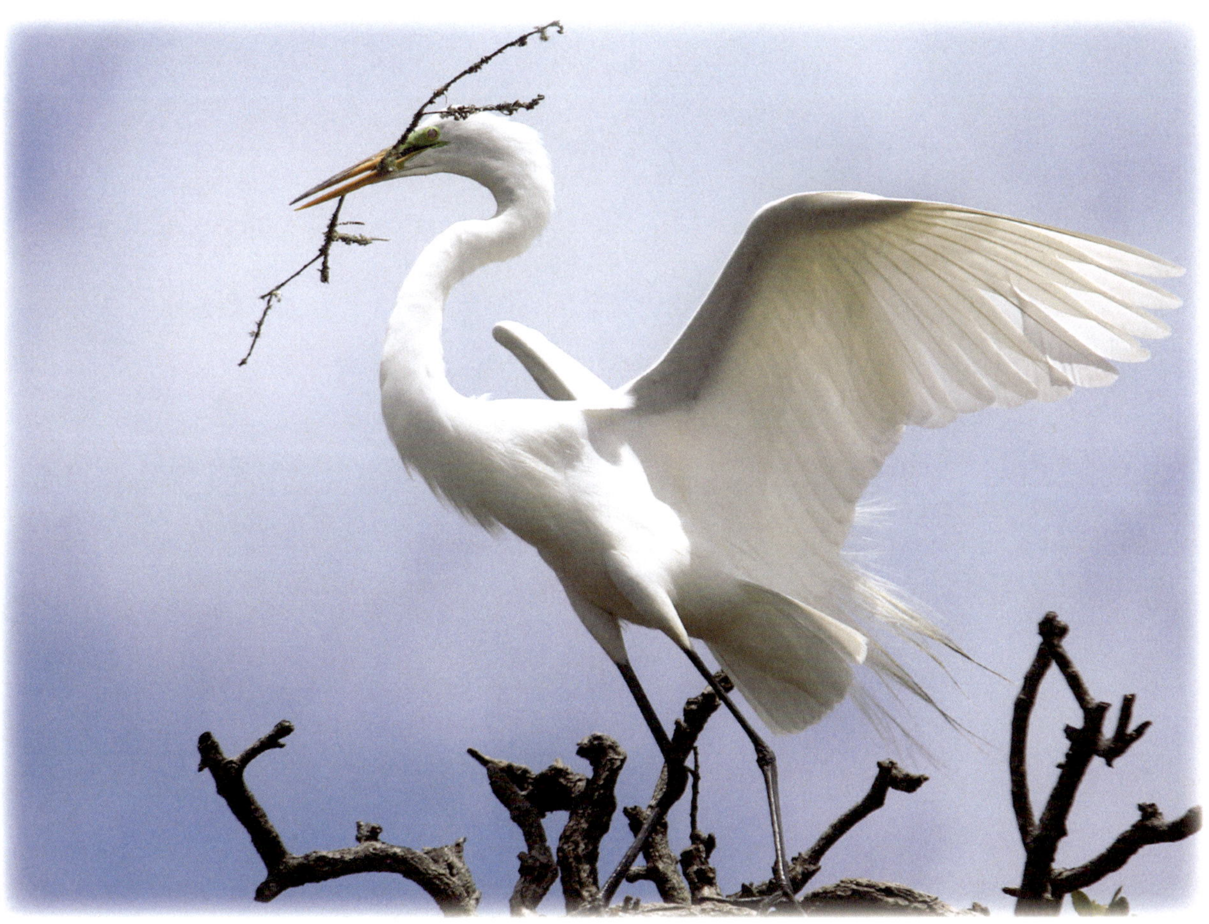

WHY PELICAN?

Brown pelicans commute early,
gliding through pink light
finding favorite fishing spots,
spending hours plummeting
head-first, feet akimbo,
neck-head-bill a spear aimed
toward fish—or crustacean,
a turtle or two—whoever may be
in the right place at the right time
for lunch. The gular pouch provides
a primitive airbag during collision.

Do pelicans envy herons standing
still and stately in knee-deep water,
snatching fish who come to them?
Was evolution playing tricks, giving
pelicans clumsy, heavy bodies and
droopy gular pouches hanging off
bills like unwanted carpet bags?

Why pelicans?

Not speed. Peregrine falcons win
(top speed 240 mph).
Pelicans…well, an ostrich runs faster
than a pelican flies, lumbering
at 30 mph. Penguins swim
faster and walk more gracefully.
Hummingbirds hover mid-air, sipping
elegantly from delicate flowers.

With peregrine, penguin, ostrich,
and hummingbird,

why pelican?

Pelicans first wandered prehistoric
Earth 30 million years ago. Eight
species today fish, swim, waddle
and fly on every continent except
Antarctica. At four feet tall, a seven
to eight feet wing span, this dinosaur
bird performs *wave-slope soaring*,
barely above water or, in well-
calculated V-formation, high
above, covering vast territories
with little effort but always knowing
the how and the why of themselves—
                     pelican.

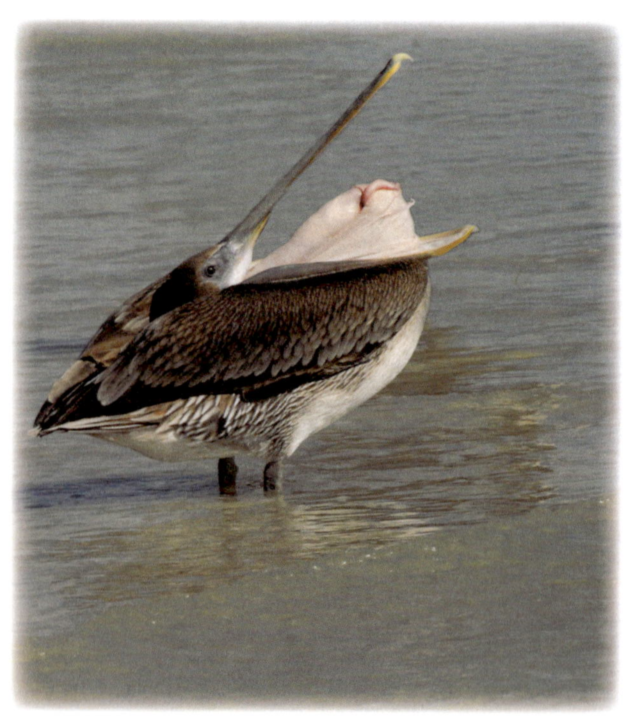

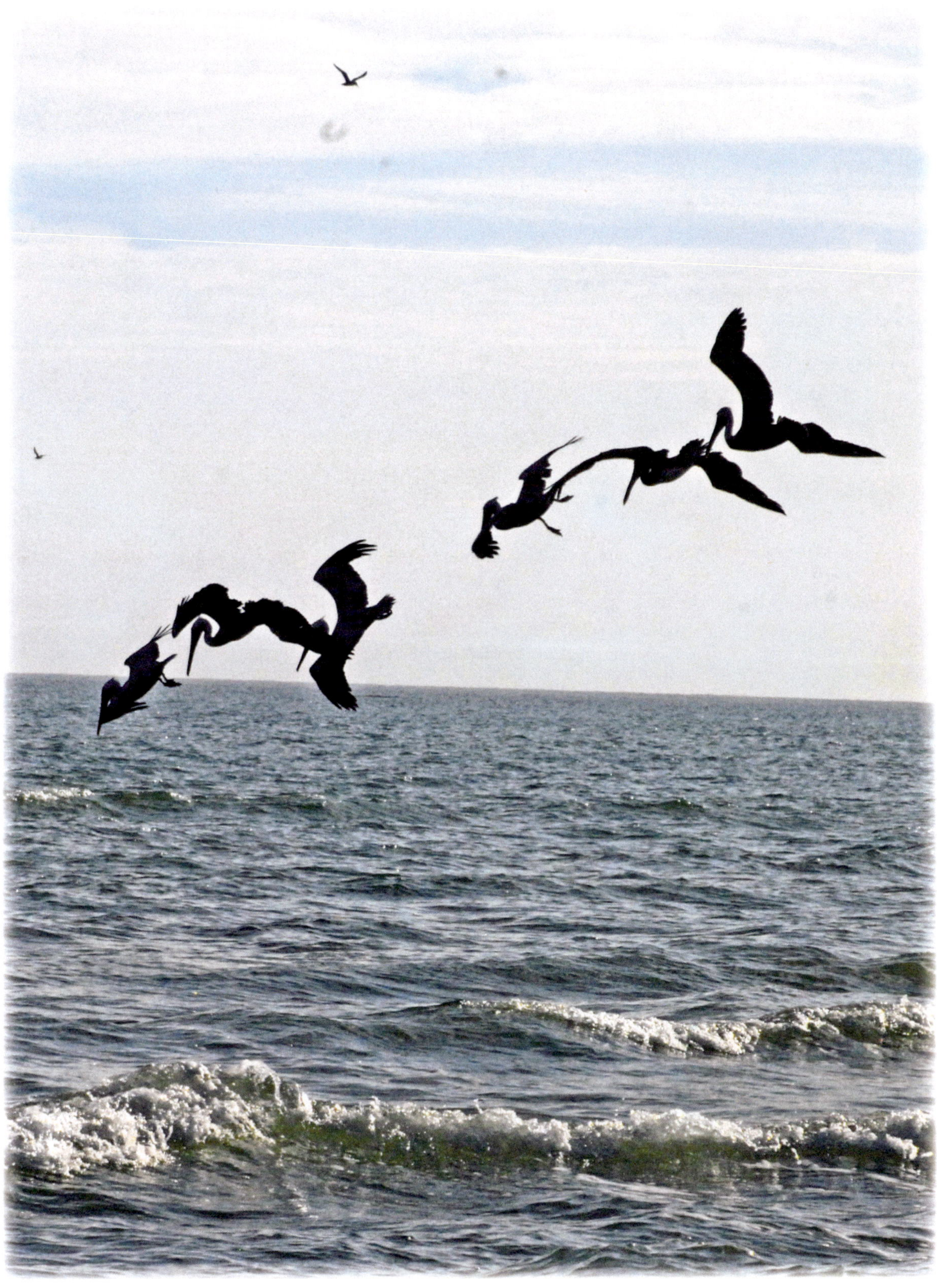

VALENTINE'S GULL

The heart is perfect
strong, persistent, focused
even if the look is …
well … off-putting…
humanly speaking
but not to another gull
    gullible in love,
      glib in voice,
        guileless in purpose.

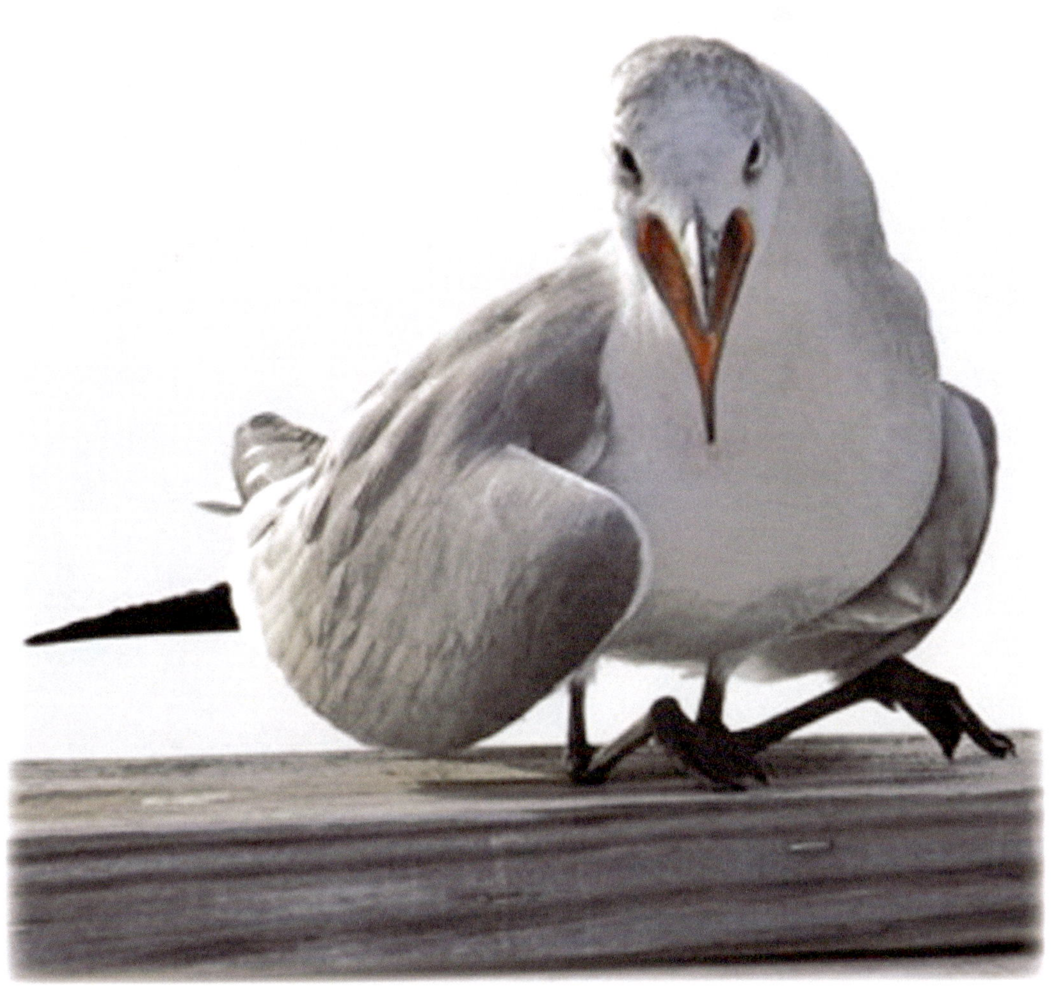

Gastropoda

Snails and slugs travel
          (slowly)
the globe. In water,
salt and fresh;
on land, in gardens,
in mountains, prairies,
and deserts. In species,
their number is vast,
estimates of 150,000 …
(only insects have more).

These abundant, traveling,
green-blooded beings
are specially known for one
vital skill: they love to eat
everything. They're
herbivorous,
carnivorous,
and detritivorous,
truly omnivorous.

So what does that mean?

They converge on gardens,
carrion, trash, even your
shoe. Anything alive or dead
will do. They'll even
excitedly merge for poo
… anyone's will do.

They find all this food
with tentacles like stalks
that move and have eyes
and the ability to sniff
out aromas no slug
could resist … they can
also follow silvery
trails of those of their
ilk leading the way to
goodies not to be missed.

Slimy and mushy and lacking
appeal, these aren't the guests
you'd invite to a meal. But
remember this: they love to eat…
everything you offer, they
appreciate. Something else
you should know: they have teeth,
          not just a few,
but thousands that wear down,
fall out and grow anew! Think
about how they can chew
your veggies, meat, leftovers, too!

They're not just pests.
They clean up our waste,
they scour out messes,
and they themselves
are food for the masses
of mammals, worms,
beetles and birds
          (to thrushes they
             especially appeal).

So a slug or two wherever
they're found belong naturally
here. They've a job to do.
Be kind. Give them a home
and maybe a dab of
tomato or poo.

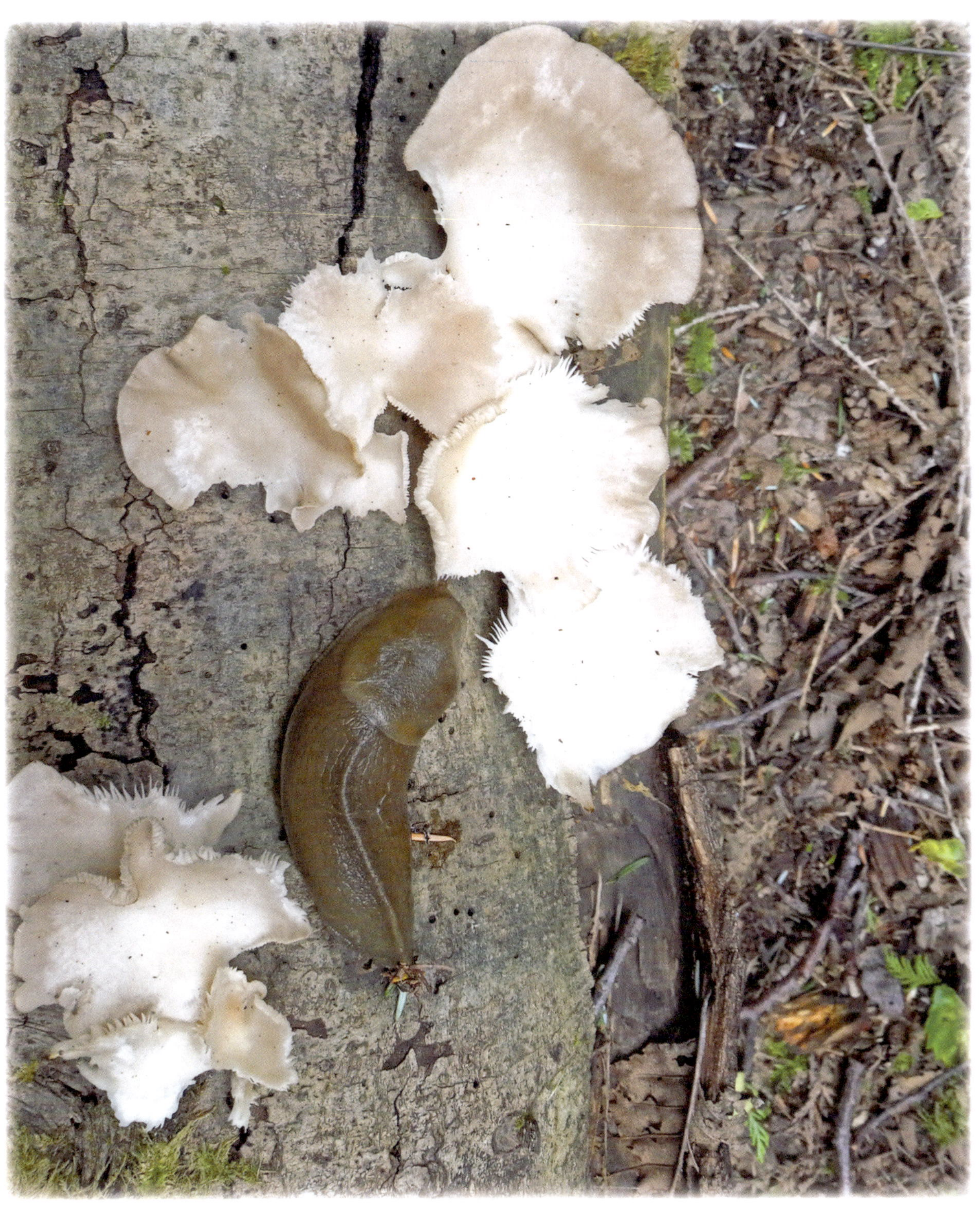

WHAT'S IN A NAME?

"A little neglect may breed great mischief."
--Benjamin Franklin

"Ferret!" shouts the child
pointing at a romp of otters.
"Ducks," says another child,
giggling at a parcel of oyster-
catchers bobbing offshore.
The adults point out crows as
ravens and hawks as falcons.
Meanwhile, "Snake!" someone
screams as a skink skitters by.

Does it matter, this blatant
confusion of species, of purpose
and need of clean water and air,
of a rainforest, bog or praire
to roam? So what if their
homes vanish into suburbs,
malls, freeways, and dumps.

If we don't know a gull
from a duck, do we care
if they're out of luck?
Besides, there's still a ferret,
a mallard or two, even a lizard,
here at our zoo!

Humans come first.
Our wants are abundant!

      Wait!

As we lose our savannas, deltas,
jungles, forests, and bogs, our
air's turning foul and our water
to poison. Is our fate linked
to the extinct and the struggling
few? Are we killing ourselves, too?

      Wow! Who knew?

***

A proverb describes neglect's cost:

For want of our care, an otter is lost.
For want of an otter, a forest is lost.
For want of a forest, our air is lost.
For want of air, all life is lost.
And all for the want of our care.

* For want of a nail, the shoe was lost.
  For want of a shoe, the horse was lost.
  For want of a horse, the rider was lost.
  For want of a rider, the battle was lost.
  For want of a battle, the kingdom was lost,
  And all for the want of a horseshoe nail."

*Benjamin Franklin included this version of the proverb,
preceded by the words, "A little neglect may breed great
mischief," in Poor Richard's Almanack in 1758.

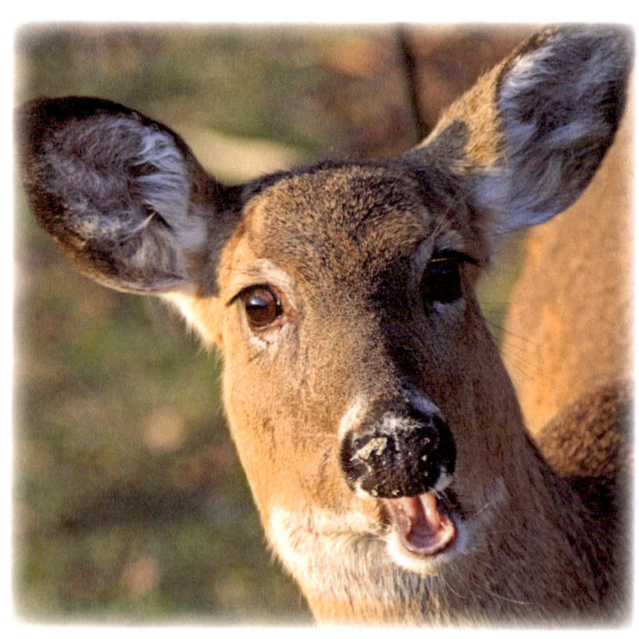

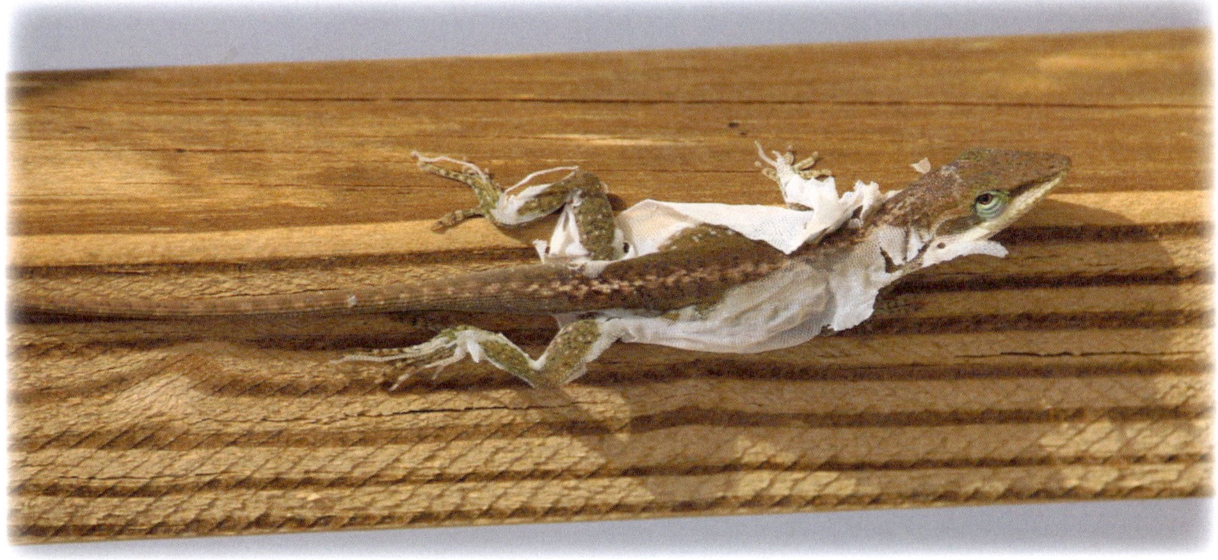

WHAT IS A MINNOW?

What a minnow is *not*
is just any glint of silver
or flash in a creek
like a wink
from a stranger.

What a minnow is *not*
is *just any*
tiny fish
or some mamma
fish's baby.

What a minnow is *not*
is always little
not all the time
just sometimes
small
and sometimes not
      not at all.

What a minnow *is*
is a fishy clan,
like trout or piranha.
Fish have babies,
some hatched
and some born live.
We call all
these infants fry.
All fry are small
and some grown
minnows
are small
but not all small
fish are minnows,
no, not at all.

What a minnow *is*
      (scientifically)
is Cyprinidae,
the largest fish family
      (3160 species
         of carp galore).
Other fish
belong to families,
too, like Salmonidae–
trout and chum–
and Serrasalmidae
–piranha and pacu–
to name a few.

What a minnow *is*
is endless surprise,
ranging from tiny
adults
–an inch or two–
to big as you:
Colorado pikeminnow
(endangered, it's true)
can be 100 pounds
and six   feet   long:
most certainly not
a silver wriggle
or flash passing by,
no, not at all.

So when a tiny
fish nibbles
your toes,
don't shout
minnow
'cause
who knows!
it might just be
piranha fry
with its mamma
nearby.

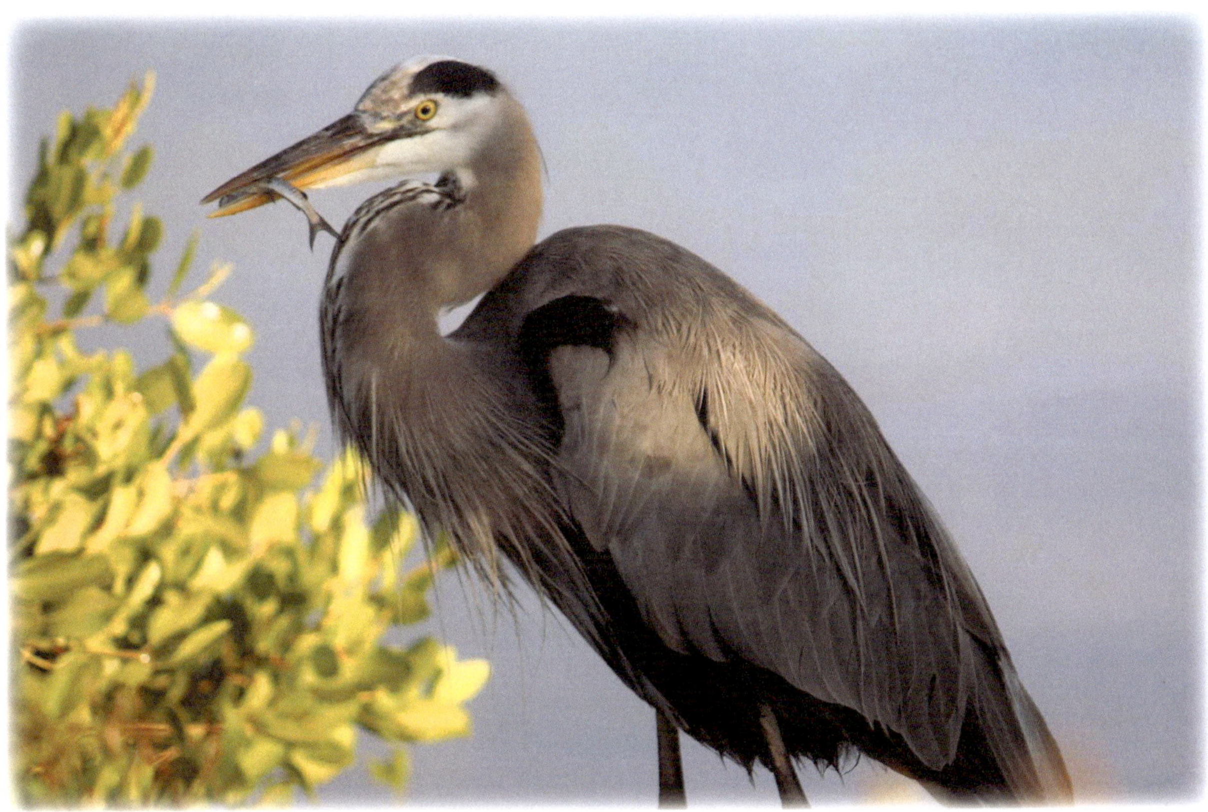

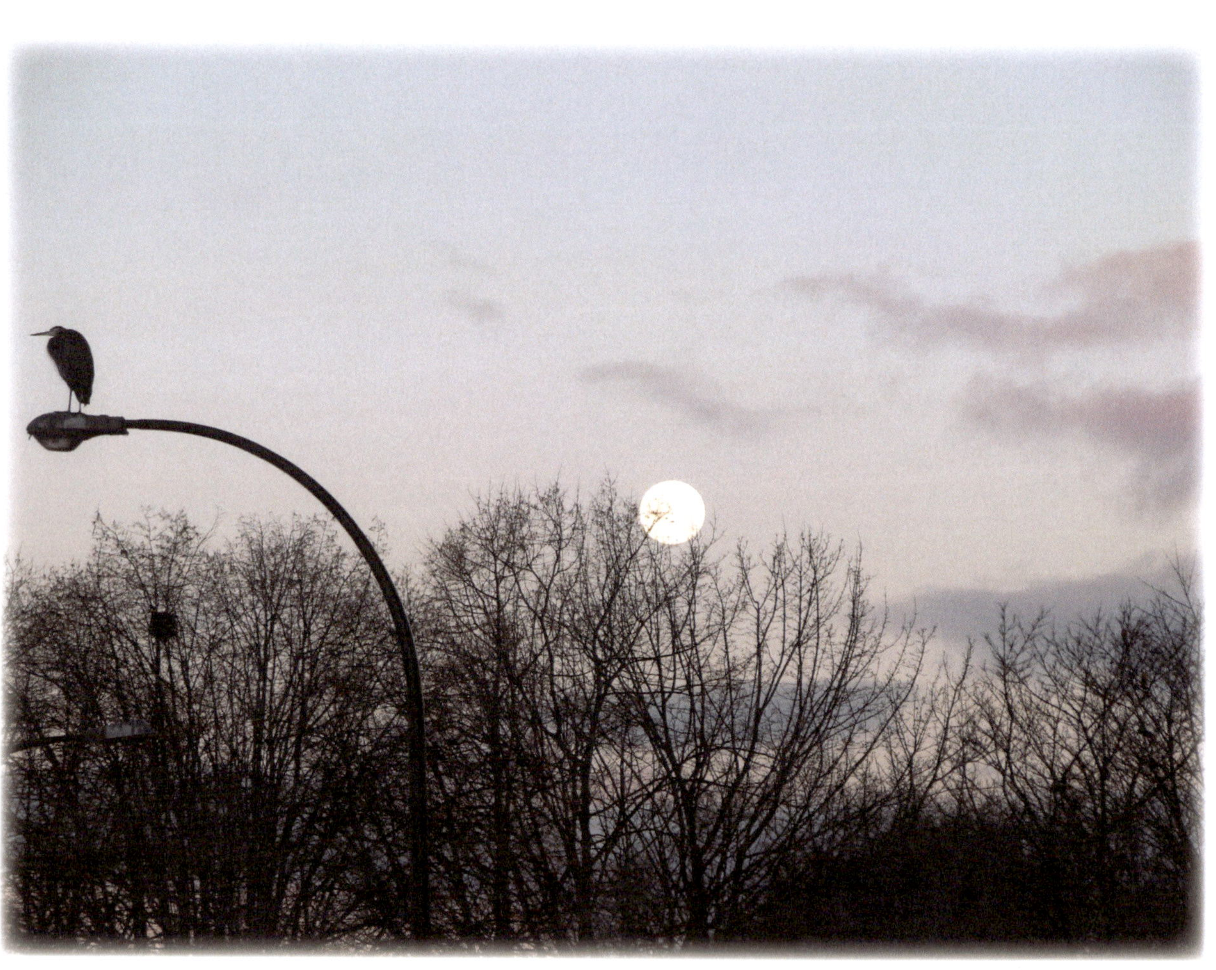

MIRRORS

"The environment, after all, is where we all meet, where we all have a mutual interest. It is one thing that all of us share. It is not only a mirror of ourselves, but a focusing lens on what we can become."

 —Lady Bird Johnson, First Lady of the United States (1963–69)

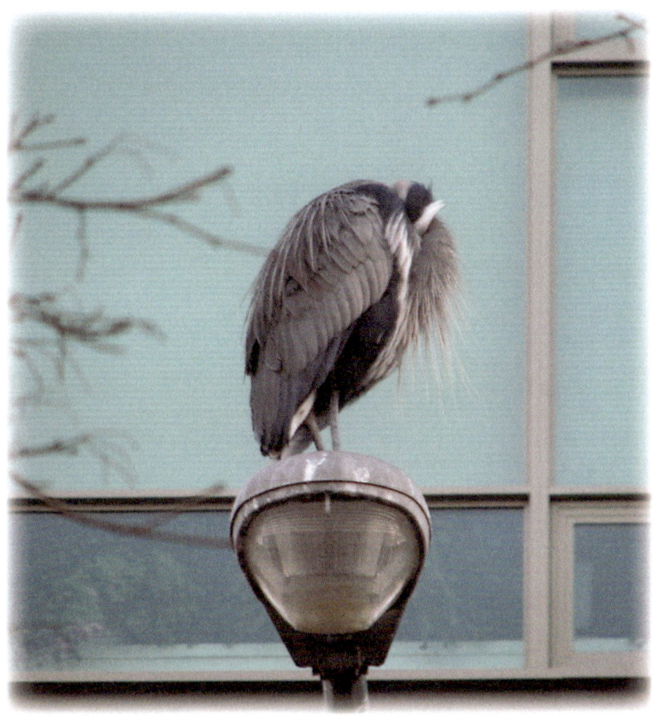

CROCODYLIDAE

deep
fossilized thoughts
you remember
other sea rises
droughts
freezes
fires
top predators
   tyrannosaurus
   homo sapiens
flash into the now,
then vanish

you remain
now and the next
180 million years
royal dominion
   in swamps
   in jungles
   in rainforests

still smiling

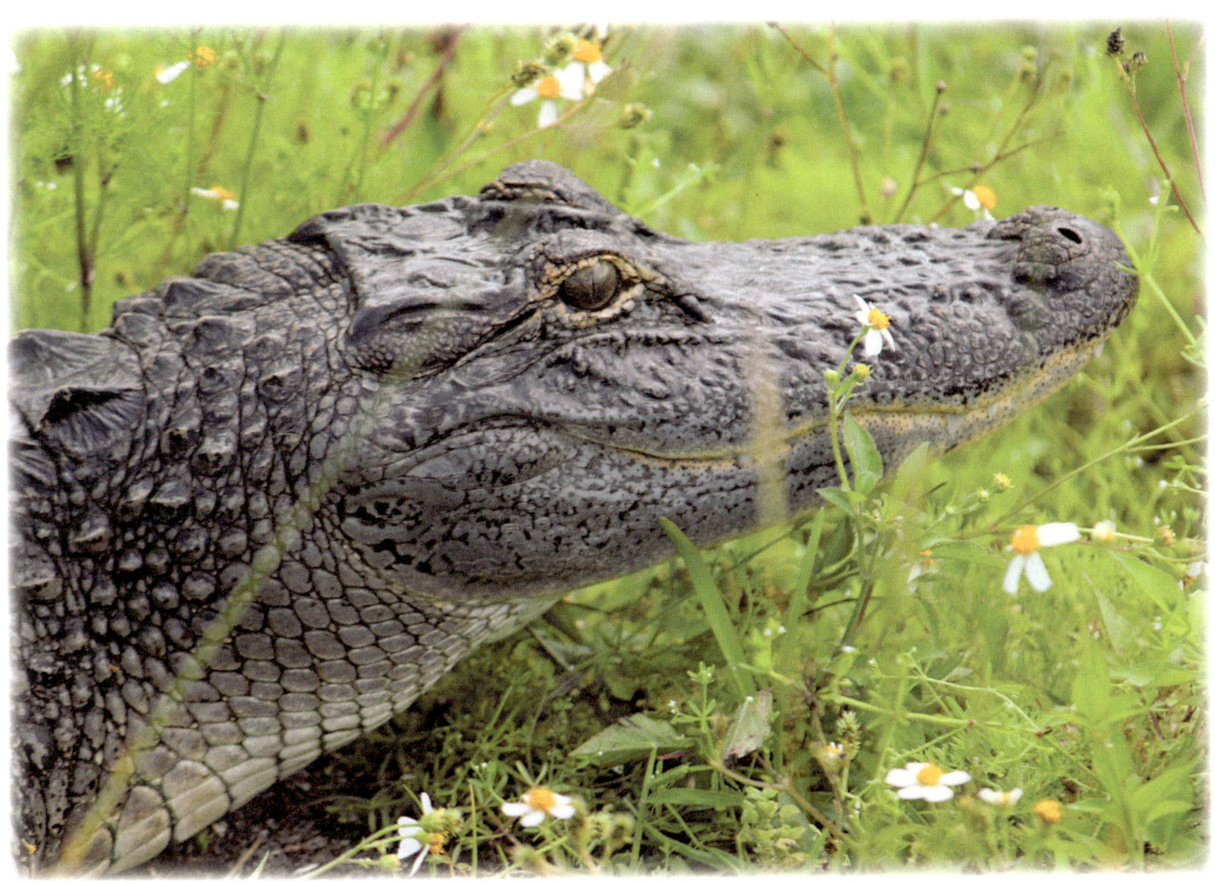

Mighty Mites

Chiggers dance on six
continents feeling
at home in nearly every
biome, skipping from
grassy slopes
to picturesque moss.
Warmer climes
are favorites. These
arachnids greet
tender flesh
        tourists preferred
        exposed in sandals
        shorts
        shirtless.

Yum.

Chiggers, just juvenile
(larval) mites
—red bugs on a romp—
latch on and when full,
slip away like cat burglars
leaving behind

flames of desire
to scratch, rub, and weep
by newly afflicted who
dance across landscapes
as if on fire.

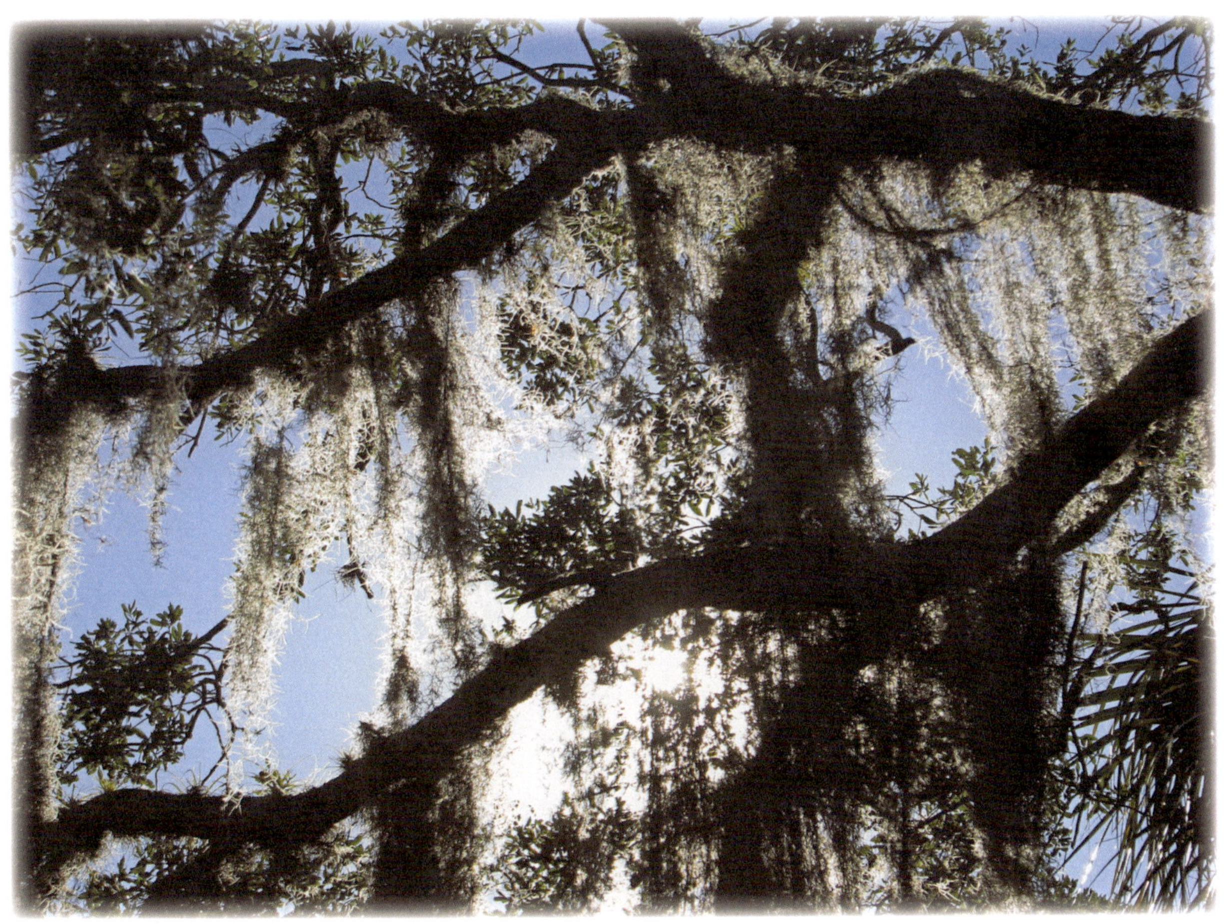

CRYSTAL RIVER

Floating.
Drifting.
The boat hull
a dull lump.
Cold water skims
my skin. I consider
retreat
to dry towels
and hot cocoa.

A sudden shadow
below.
Then gone, vanished
in tannin-stained
water.

Another shadow
surfaces,
brushes me,
dives.
Many shadows
become solid,
soft-eyed and whiskered.

My rules:
not to touch,
not to dive
not to chase
not to interfere
with endangered and ancient
creatures.
Even dangling
a rope can later lure
trusting creatures
to their death, tangled
in crab pots or
next to whirling
prop knives.
One-thousand
pounds
of vulnerability.

So I remain
passive,
breathless,
encased in manatees
—sea cows, sirens, mermaids, dugong—
bumping, crowding, touching,
breaking my rules.

The need for air
overwhelms
my breath-holding wonder.
My snorkel rattles.
I resist any urge
to move. Chills slide
away. I'm suspended
with elephant cousins
pre-dating my
human ancestors
by fifty million years.

Manatee request
nothing
but time and space to graze
peacefully on plants.
Only humans
neglect
the request.

The river weeps
droplets into my mask
that mix with salt.
We drift toward
our mother sea.

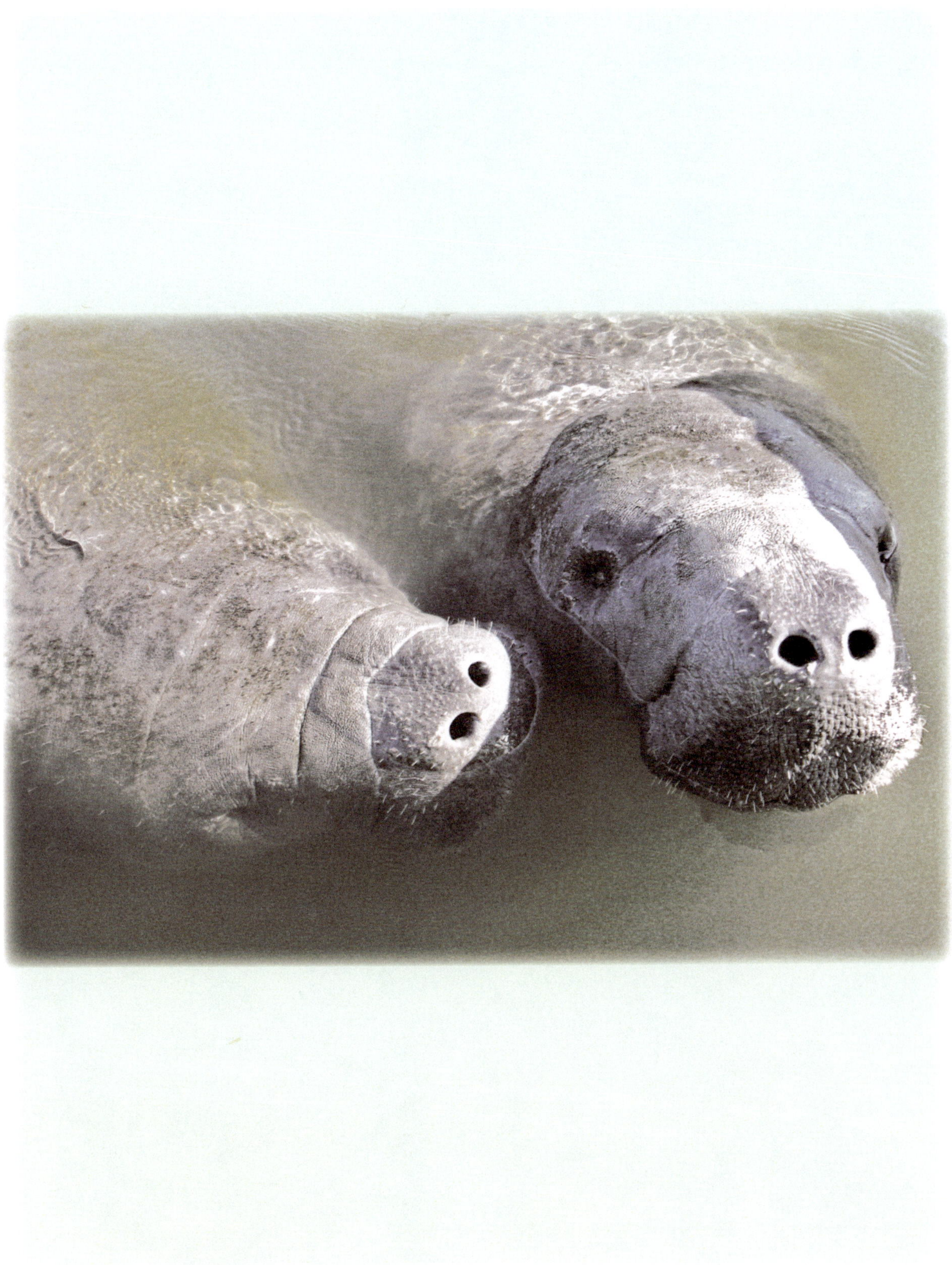

CATCHING FISH

isn't easy
and requires flair
whether done
from land, water
or air. Yet, many
mammals and birds,
crustaceans and fish
choose pescatarian
fare. Critters
who fish learn to be
versatile, using
various styles:
plunging
running
darting
skimming
chasing
upending
and just splashing around
          for a while.

Some dive
from great heights;
some dive
from the surface;
some swim
and some don't…
some just stand
on the land.

Some hunt alone,
some fish in a group.
Some humpback whales
blowing bubbles galore,
create a great net.
Some seals herd fish
into dead end bays.
Some, use sticks, poles,
or paws—or even bait—
to capture their dinner. *
Some just lie in wait.**
Some—birds, otters
and crabs, too—use
rocks as hammers
on shellfish dinners.
Some birds drop shells
from great heights;
isn't that wild?

Perhaps we humans
could learn a lot
by watching critters
and the skills that
they've got.

* Hank heron "Smart heron uses bread as bait for fishing,
BBC

** Alligator

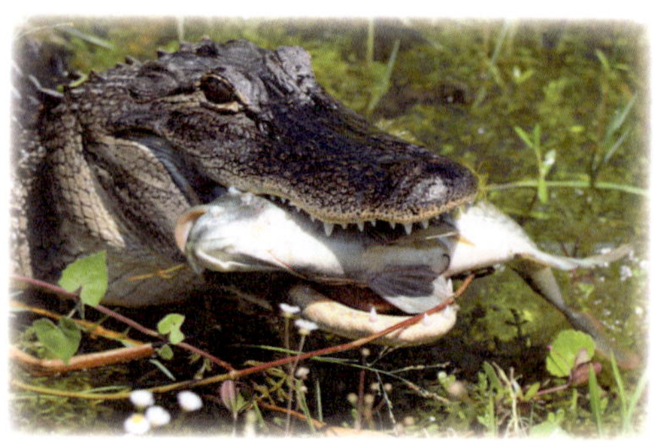

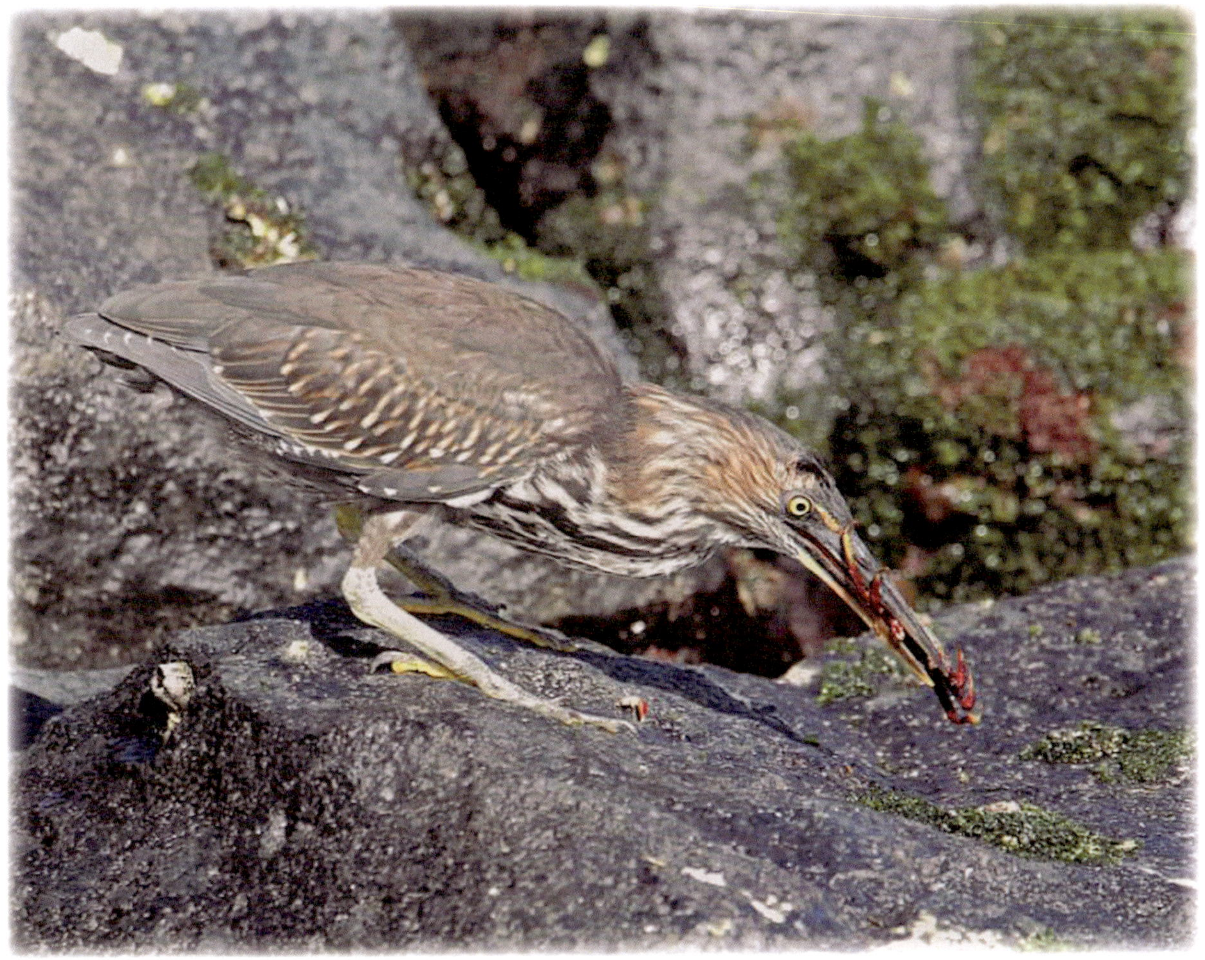

PHRAGMITES

Some call it bulrush,
rush for short,
or even reed,
grass, and weed.
Then we've
cattails and sedges,
not to mention
native and not;
ohmygosh, what
are they not?

They're not rare—
they're everywhere!
They grow well
where nothing
else can. If soil
and water are foul,
they don't care ...
they'll clean it up,
locking away carbon,
arsenic, mercury,
and such creating
sustainable living,
welcome to all.*

Abundantly useful
phragmites are for
more than just clean
water and air. They
serve for arrows
and flutes, blow
guns and thatch,
matting and knives ...
certainly phragmites
have brightened
our lives, especially
in evening when
reddening sun
sparks on seed tips
flaming like fire.

*Pragmites, especially those nonnative, can be detrimental to native vegetation

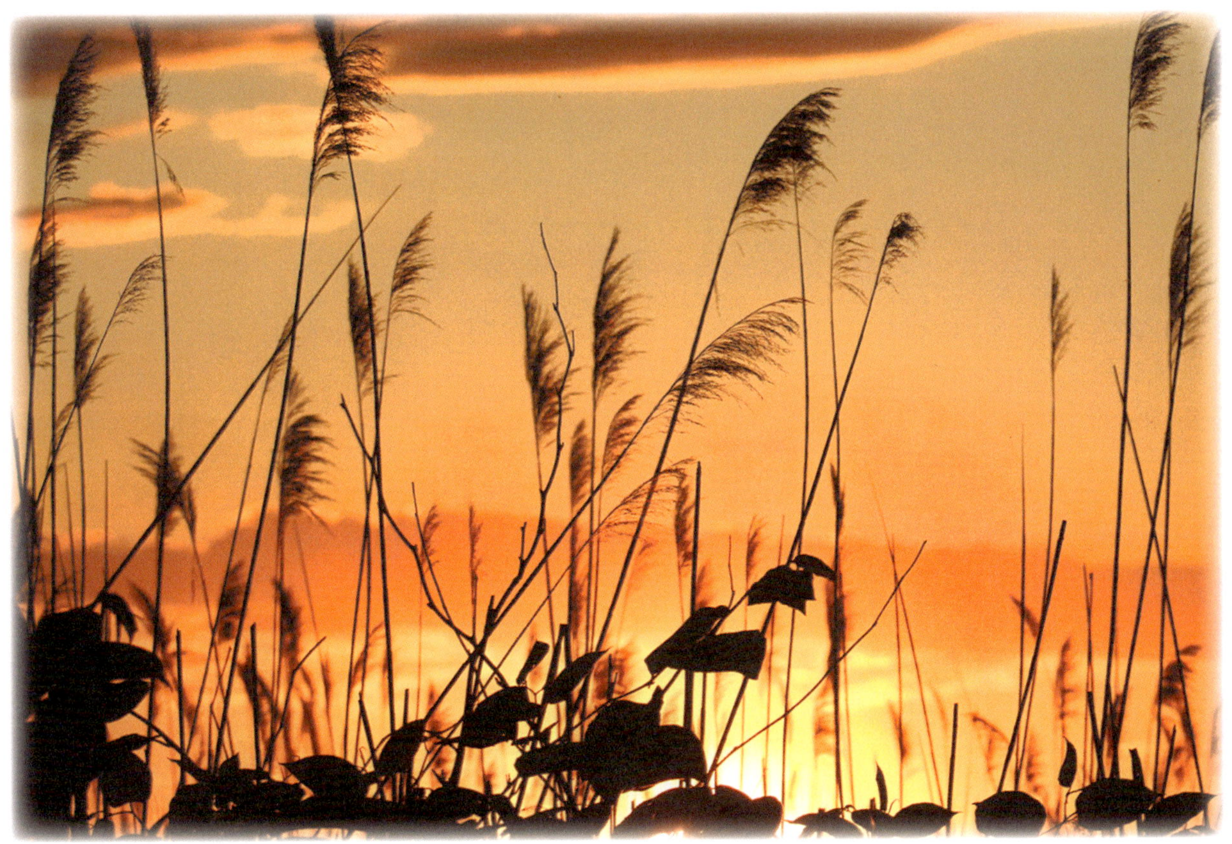

INVADERS

Not aliens,
exactly,
they arrive
by boat
by car
by wind
by sea currents
from anywhere on Earth
not on purpose,
not willing
always.

Scooped into barrels,
attached to hulls
of wandering ships,
nested in timber,
stowaways,
unwelcome guests
on ferries, trains, planes
crossing oceans
and continents.

They appear
in underwear drawers,
in gardens,
in Los Angeles elevators.

We know them,
recognize them,
possibly *like* them.
We buy them
curse them, pet them,
kill them, smuggle them,
free them into swamps.

Coyotes in town.
Eastern grey squirrels
in western forests.
Burmese pythons
in Florida wetlands.
Asian carp in Europe.
Cane toads in Australia.
European starlings –
　　　　everywhere.
Rabbit and kudzu
and mongoose...

These aliens,
these invaders,
take over
unexpected Edens.
Native species
suffer predation
or starvation again
illustrating how well
humans mismanage
Earth.

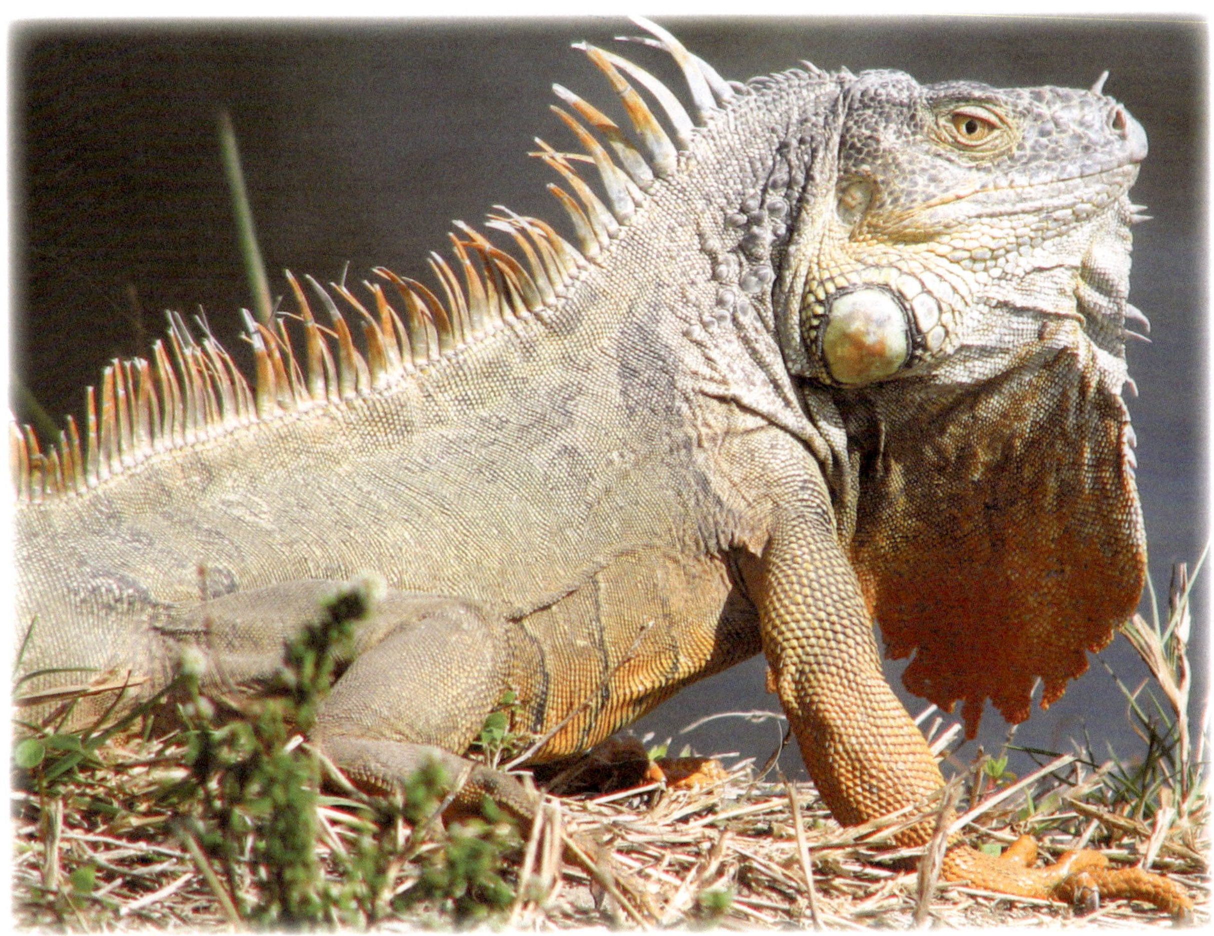

Cloudy Thinking

All that data amongst the Cloud
Nine for the Internet, invisible
waves that exist, or not, depending
on philosophy, storms, or luck.

Social survival relies on cloudy lists
of life's details, a substitute little
black book and secretary; friends
and family contact numbers,
passwords, birthdays, anniversary
parties and dental appointments.

We think we're clever inventing
external brains clouded with details
we access with a touch or a word
or lose, maybe forever, when
clouds disperse and drought ensues.

Yet, our Web is eons behind
spidery webs providing extended
cognition (we don't understand)
about when and how the spinner
can complete tasks for dinner.*

Other creatures, too, extend brain
functions beyond the expected.
Octopodes (octopuses or octopi
for some) embrace brains (literally)
in their arms. Fungi (funguses for some
but fungoid not so much) and trees
share information and resources
as outreach through soil. Many
insects and aquatic dwellers have
little or no brain at all, not that we
can decode, no, not even with our
Cloud, yet their functions work fine,
never needing to be turned off, then on
again to reboot their *how-to* senses.
Other processes, too, are sometimes
outsourced: Insects might *hear*
through their thoraces, wings, or legs.

Next time you turn to the Cloud to find
your schedule, your password, or your
Mom's telephone number, consider
the Web of the spider or the brainless
sponge who function perfectly with
extended cognition we can't quite
envision even if our global Web helps
us wonder, finally, about what to wonder.

*https://www.quantamagazine.org/the-thoughts-of-a-spiderweb-20170523/

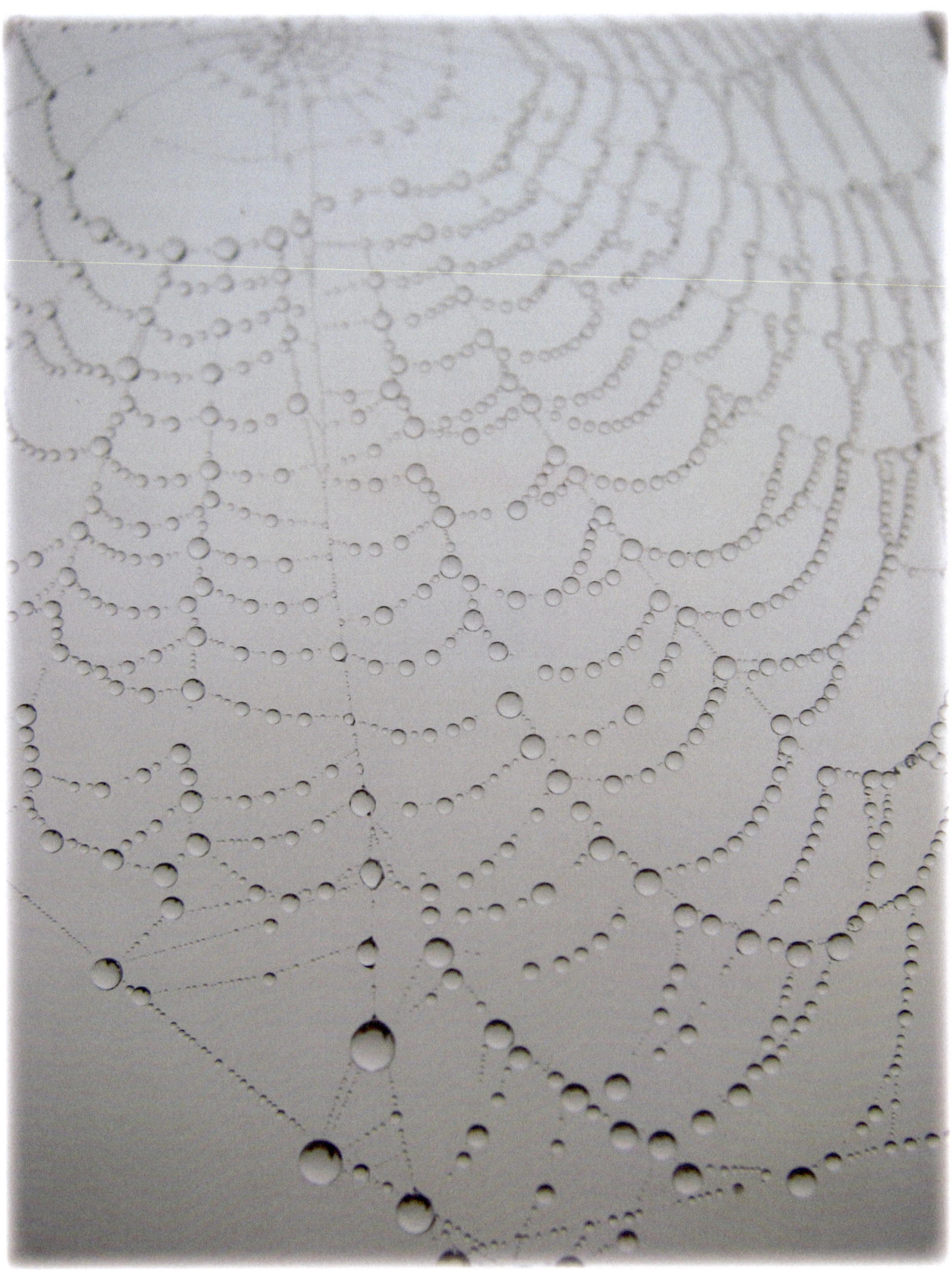

FLORIDA BEACHFRONT

Florida beaches stretch and yawn for miles,
embracing Florida with breaking waves
tossing rainbow mist to soaring pelicans.
Seeking a tropical glow, thong-clad people
lounge and prowl sandy stretches, from surf
to city where sand dives under concrete.

Sand emerges where pavement breaks,
where cultivated gardens grow thin,
within flatwood landforms boasting
the most aquods* in the United States.
Sandy, too, is Florida's unique state soil,
Myakka, often called "sand" by those
not knowing *this* soil from *that* soil.

Even Britton Hill, Florida's peak point,
elevation three-hundred forty-five feet—
the lowest state high point in the USA—
plants itself atop sand, "laying out"
beneath Florida sun while Alabama,
only a minute away, gazes lustily at the clear
flaunting of this lofty mound. Tourists
flock to climb this low high point, heeding
the local warning from Estus Whitfield,
"If you get light-headed and dizzy,
sit down and breathe deep for a few
minutes before going higher."

Sliding downhill, Myakka covers more
than a million and a half acres populated
by tourists and wild boars,
orchids and carnivorous pitcher plants,
red-cockaded woodpeckers and gallinules,
gopher tortoises, frosted flat-woods
salamanders, and, yes, striped newts.

Call it beach. Call it wet. Call it Florida
where all property sports sandy, wet views,
and beach thoughts of breaking surf echo
coast to coast, east to west, north to south,
on slowly sinking, ever wetter real estate.

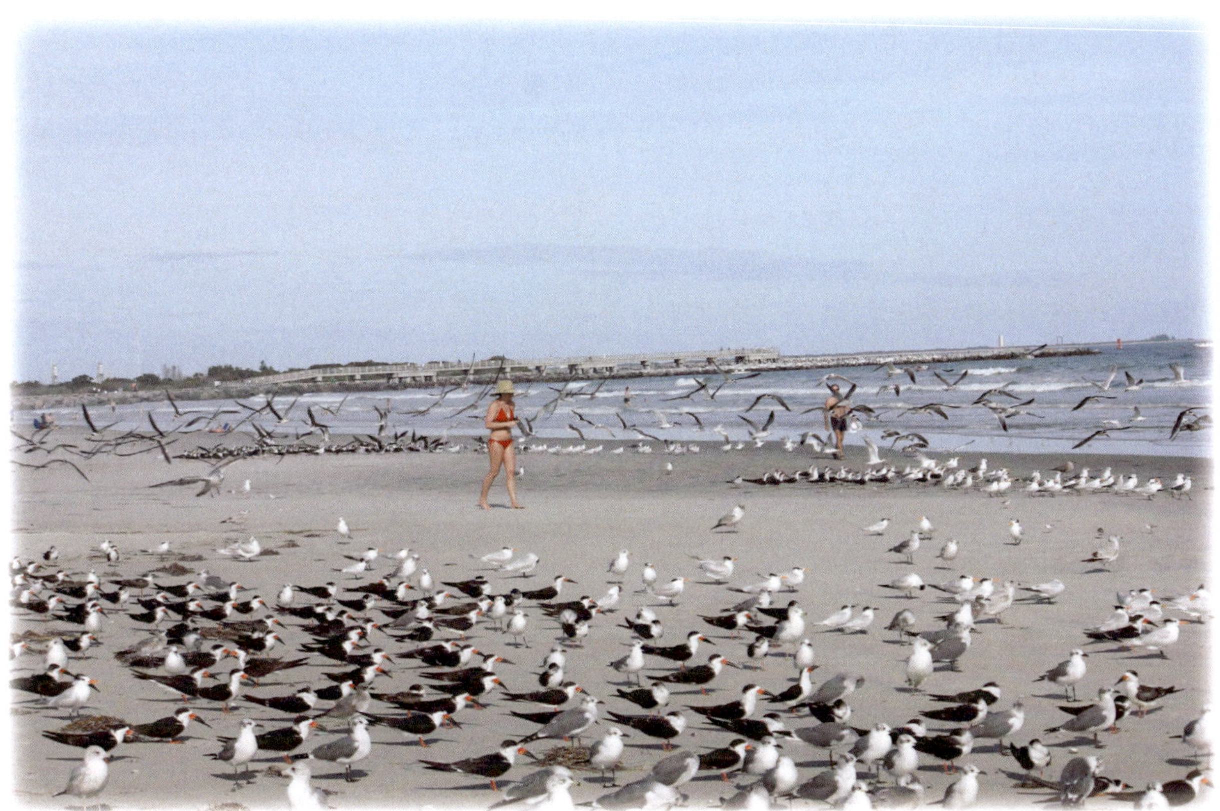

*The state of Florida has the largest total acreage of Aquods (wet, sandy soils with an organic-stained subsoil layer) on flatwood landforms in the nation. Myakka (pronounced My-yakah) is a Native American word for Big Waters, is a native soil, and is exclusive to Florida. The most extensive soil in the state, it occurs on more than 1½ million acres. Both Aquods and Myakka belong to the soil type Spodosols. On May 22, 1989, Governor Bob Martinez signed Senate bill number 524 into law, making Myakka Florida's Official State Soil.

Viera Wetlands

Arrive before
Atlantic sun skims wave crests golden
owls return to burrows
gator roars subside to lurks
sudden song scrolls bright
  through green and brown swamp
  and reedy wetlands where grebes,
  and purple gallinules gather
in Monet-scapes of weavy-water.

Stay through
  sparking pink and yellow and long-necked
  silhouettes stalking
  feeding fish and into
  afternoon stillness
    that polishes weavy-water
    to mirrors doubling trees, reeds, clouds
    and wings: soaring birds bring
late meals to nests.

Remain just
  a bit longer until pink again
  flashes into twilight buzzing insects,
  humming with enthusiastic flurry.
    Prey-seeking predators become
    prey for night swimmers and flyers.

T

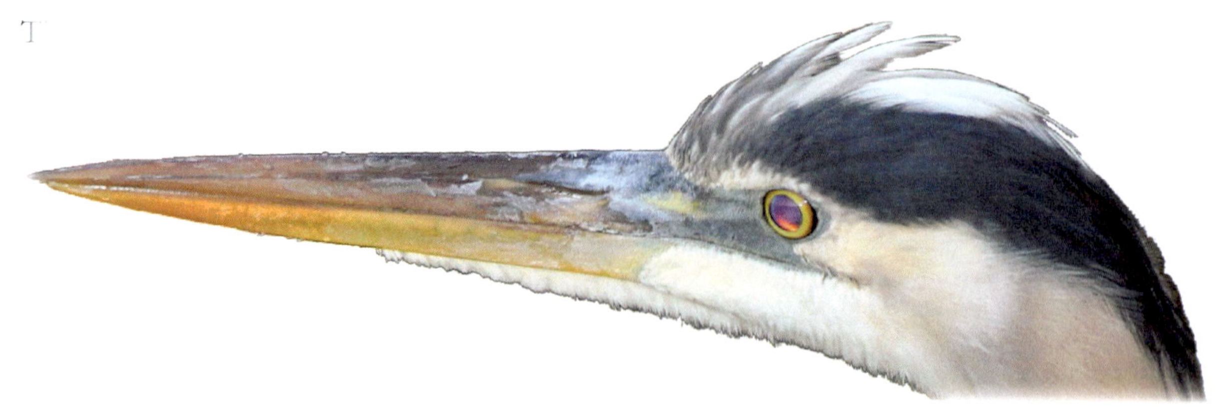

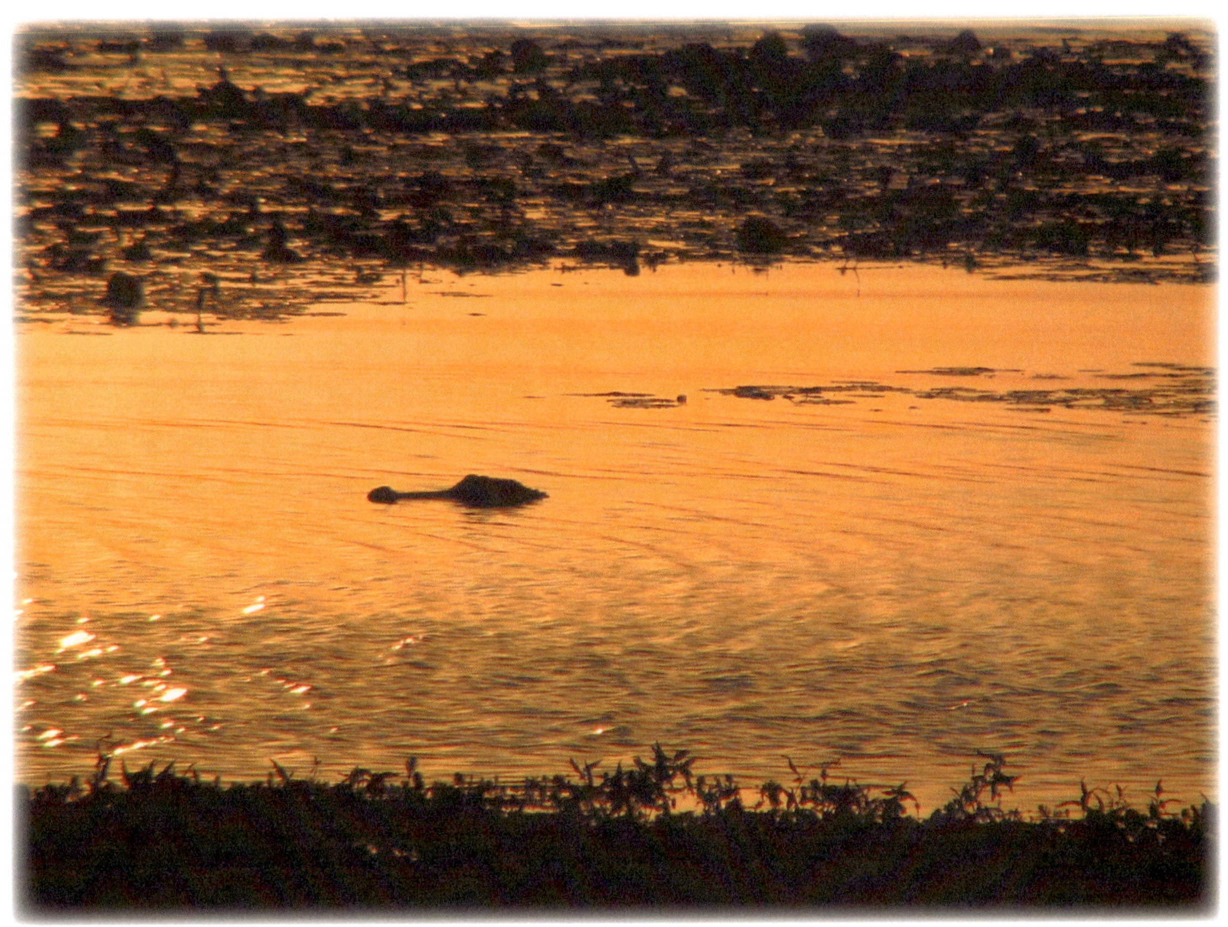

No Application Needed

for this perfect job on
recently established
sanctuary, 76 acres,
pristine wetlands, open
during daylight hours.

Hours 24/7, no salary
but board and room
if you find the board
and build the room.

No benefits
but guaranteed
place and space
for life or as long
as you care to stay.

But you're free to
fly or swim or walk
away or hide
camouflaged
in brush, mud, water
or lovely holes in snags.

Arrive on your schedule.
No vacation, no time
off, no sick days, no
holidays. Just living
life in the perfect job.

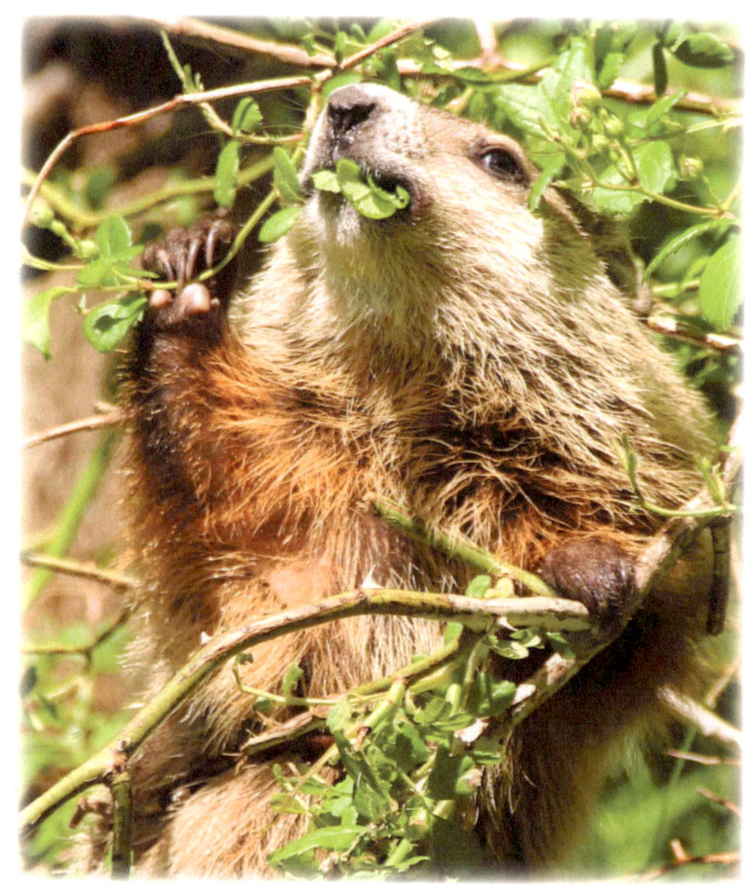

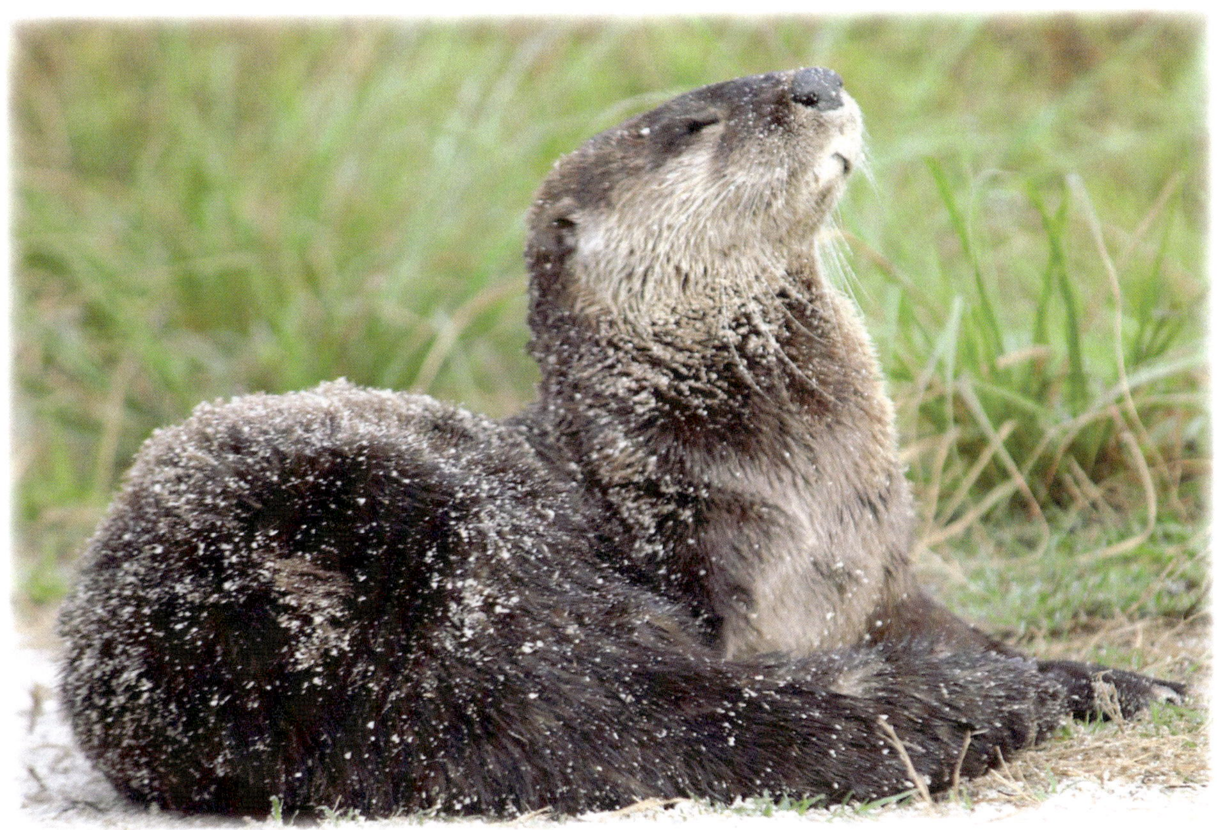

Clouds

We name them in stories,
our imagination, songs,
and academic studies.
Dragons. Barking dogs.
Ghost Riders in the Sky.
Mammatus. Cumulous.

We've risen above and
through them. We've
gazed at their cottony
mountains our passing
rips apart. With our
passing, they magically
reform, like any real
spirit, leaving intact our
beliefs in giant castles
in beanstalk valleys.

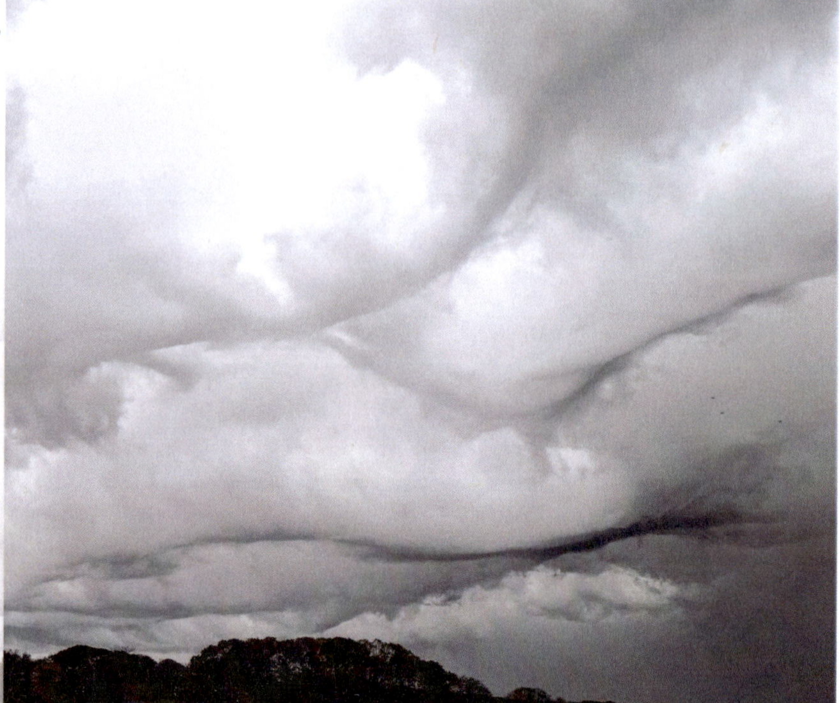

Our minds are clouded
and sometimes we walk
on Cloud Nine. Our worst
fears have the silver lining
of the darkest clouds; our
vital data securely resides
mystically in a Cloud.

Poets have found clouds
lonely or looming, like love
gone awry, changing as do
clouds from legend to
tragedy from tranquil
lambs in green pastures
to promises of worse
just beyond the horizon.

Clouds carry water droplets
old as Earth. They bring
rainbows to some and a long
awaited drink to others. They
water our crops and carry
deadly ice. They ramble
the globe, indifferent
and familiar spirits keeping
our hopes, dreams, fears,
and imaginations alive.

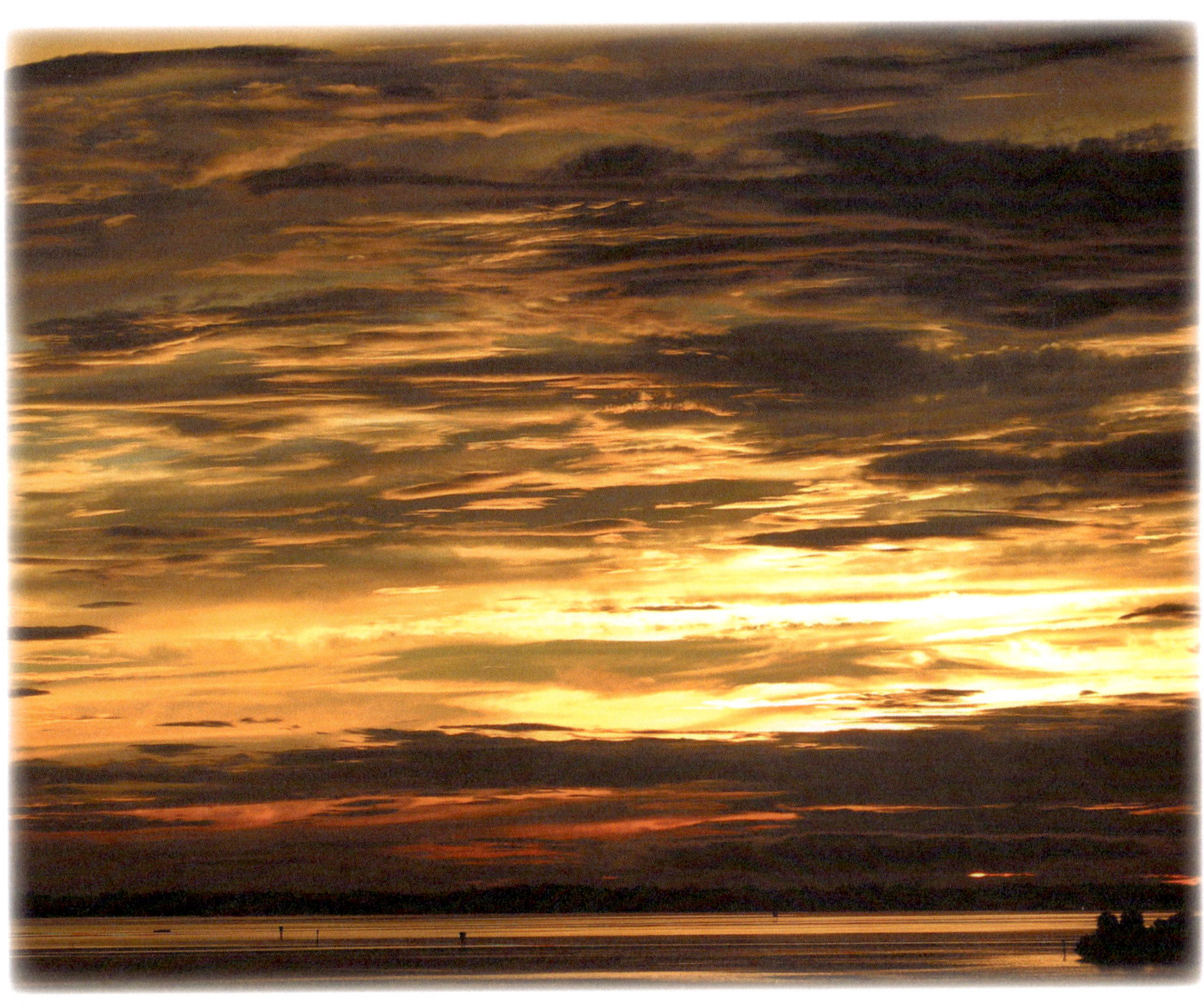

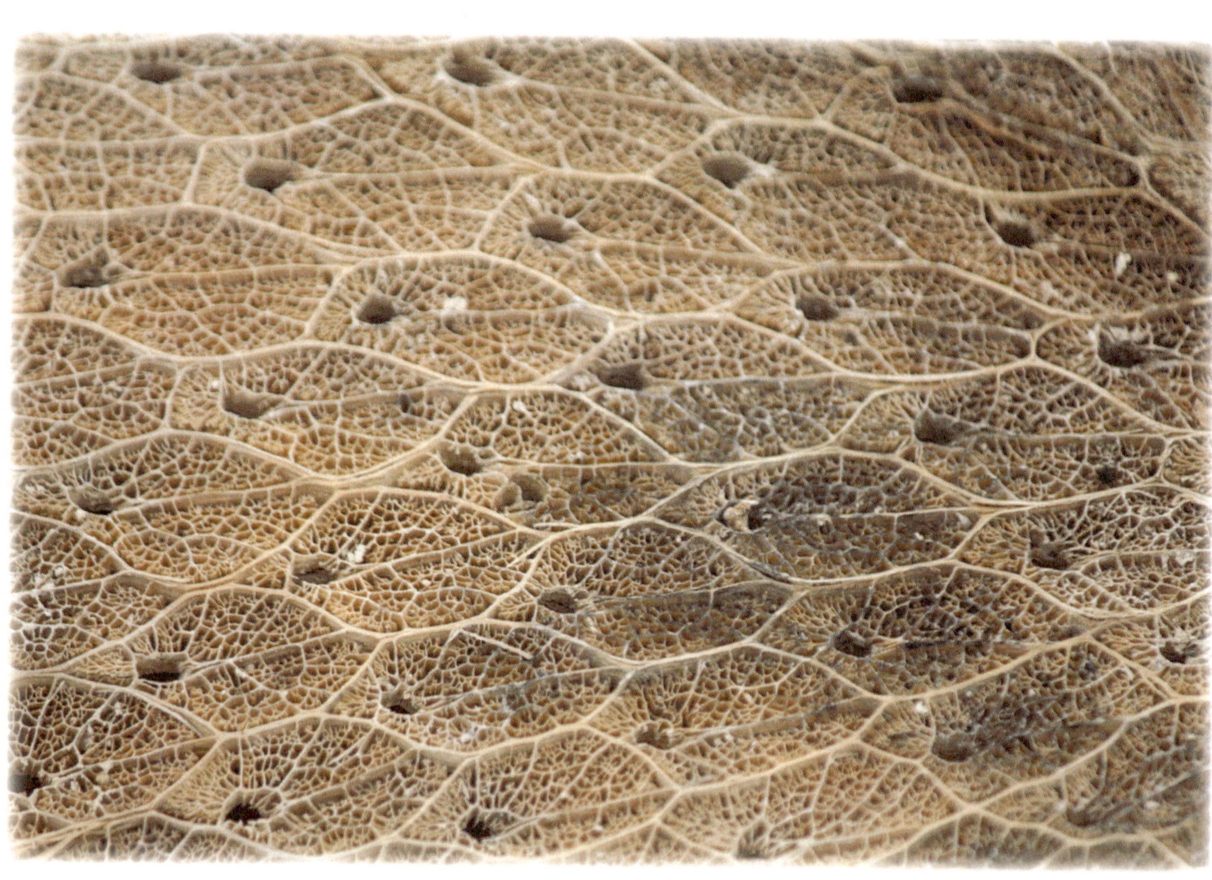

QUESTIONS

"The wilderness holds answers to questions [we have] not yet learned to ask."

– Nancy Newhall

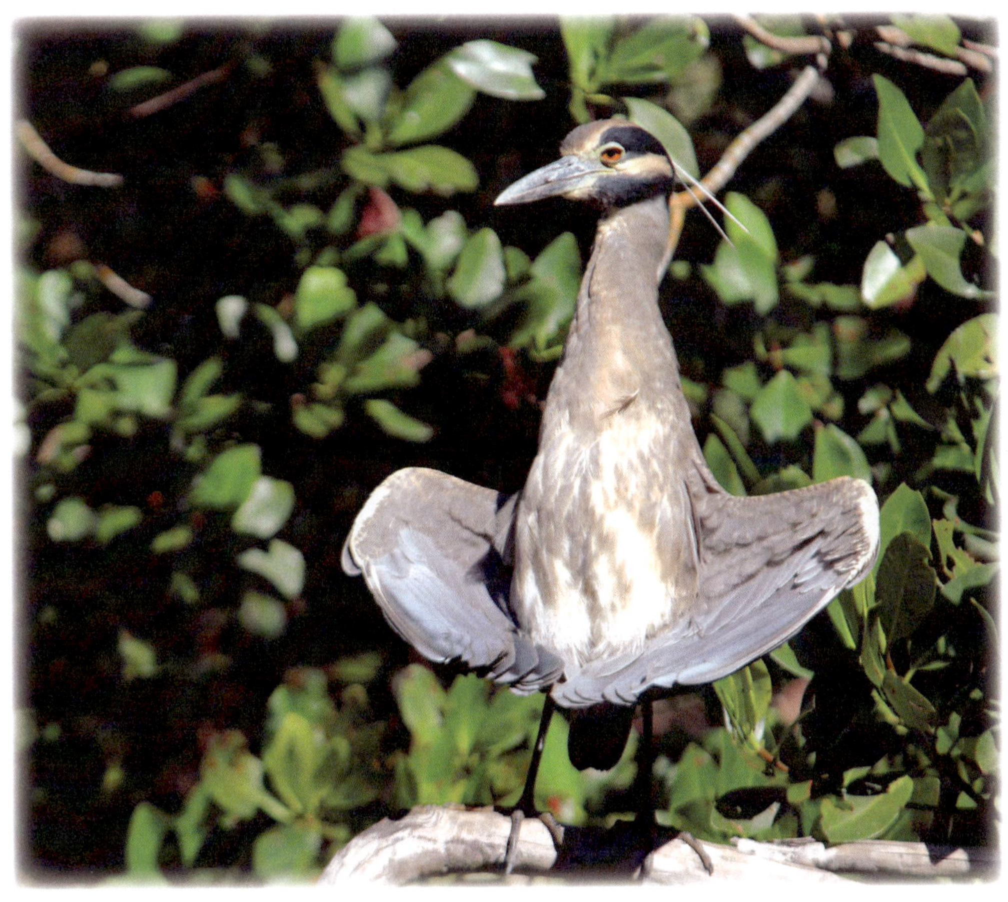

BERGS

Like icebergs floating in the sea, mountains
float on Earth's mantle with greater mass
below than above, maintaining balance.
Icebergs can flip should a balance point
shift, but mountains melt slowly, aging
from water and wind into gentler slopes.

Earth's thickest crust builds like a callus
beneath highest points; semi-molten
mantle loans material to the crust
building. Yet, loans have limits restricting
how high mountains grow just as iceberg
height depends on nine-tenths of its mass
hiding below the surface of the sea.

Sun and water conspire to carve ice
that calves, giving birth to bergs that crash
into the sea where they drift, frozen
floating islands, sometimes for millennia,
before becoming one with the sea.

For mountains, plate tectonics and fire
conspire. Massive, irregularly-shaped
slabs, plates of rock *floating* on denser
and heavier rocks below slip, collide
and break. Magma can explode upward,
flow and then, like refreezing ice, become
rock, building dome mountains peacefully
waiting to explode again. Or plates
collide, jam and fold Earth into piles
of rock and soil for spectacular
effects like the Himalayas building
to twenty-four thousand feet above sea
level. Sometimes plates just break and massive
blocks of Earth separately rise and fall,
giving birth to fault-block mountains like
California's Sierra-Nevada.

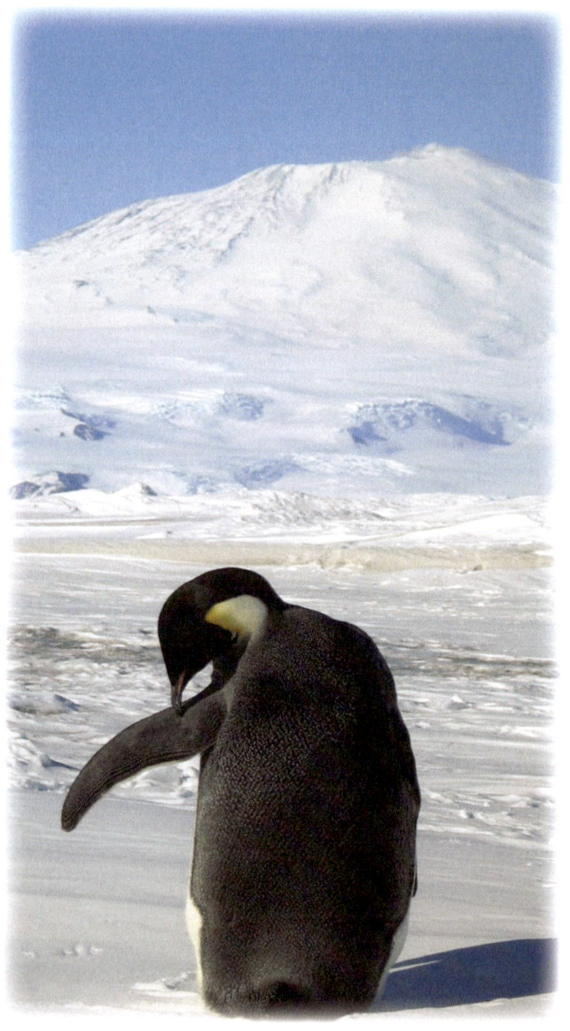

Icebergs, often striped dark from nutrients
and minerals gathered on land, vary
from massive islands to bergy bits
and growlers. Large bergs develop caves
and platforms as ice waltzes through the sea,
spewing nutrients, fertilizing tiny
photosynthetic plankton, the foundation
of the marine food web. Nutrient rich
trails can stretch hundreds of miles behind
drifting bergs. Massive iceberg keels stir
water, adjust salinity, support
algae and krill, bristle worms, and fish.
Seabirds, seals, and penguins use ice for rest
and for its traveling food buffet. Life
and death combine to spawn organic
detritus, trapped carbon drifting down
to the sea bottom for cold storage.

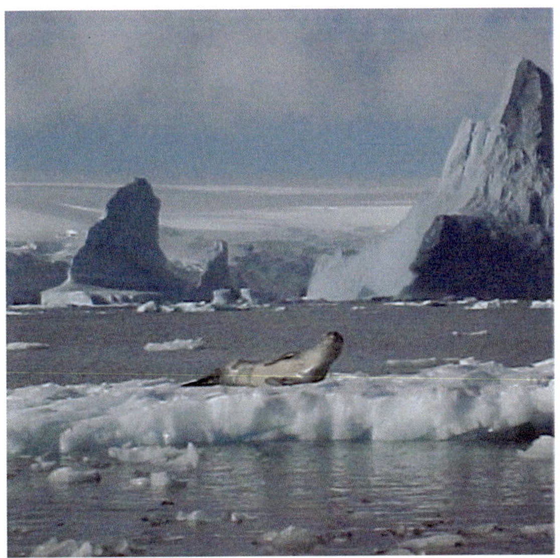

Mountains build ecosystems in place.
Rising from low elevations to high,
they create weather, wringing moisture
from rising air, changing ecosystems,
from foothills to alpine, along the way.
Cresting the mountain, air, now colder
and dryer, flows downhill, creating
ecosystems dramatically different
from the slope facing prevailing winds.
Water and wind and even lava flow,
create caves and valleys, provide
diverse homes for quirky creatures such as
American pikas on talus slopes
and Galapagos penguins in lava tubes.
Mountains even change human politics
with natural borders difficult to cross.

Yet even the most massive, the most
solid, remains vulnerable. Earth:
alive, ever creative, ever changing,
challenging everything she shelters —
adapt, evolve, protect, and revere.

UPSIDE DOWN

My childhood classrooms
posted pictures of upside
down food chains putting
predators atop a pyramid,
dominating everything else.

And so we would ask,
"What good is it?" before
spraying, smashing,
    shooting, trapping,
        toppling, bulldozing
            eating, or poisoning it.

Who had a better question?

"What good is it?" we'd ask
when gazing at free-running
rivers, towering mountains,
500-year old trees. When *it*
failed to answer, we damned
rivers, leveled mountains
and trees, paved wetlands,
and built factories puffing
out toxic smoke to make
toxic stuff we defined
as useful, stuff to stuff
in stores, garages, attics,
basements, and endless self-
storage units; stuff we
couldn't eat, stuff we couldn't
wear, stuff we couldn't use
to improve conditions for
other members of the food
web we didn't know existed.

Since those distant days,
we abandoned the chain,
toppled the pyramid, saw
predators as just one more
group on various food webs
for many ecosystems.

Predators—and most certainly
humans—we've come to know
are dependent, not dominant,
on Earth; dependent for survival
on clean air and water (which
we can't make), on toxic-free
soil (which we can't make),
on pollinators (which we can't
make), on grazers, and more.
                Who knew?

We've discovered answers
to our question: soil microbes
help produce food for plants
that provide food for grazers.
Insects pollinate those plants.
Trees provide shelter, food,
shade and clean air. Is every-
thing good for something?

But the question, "What good
is it?" continues to haunt us
when we try to fix the broken
rivers, the vanishing forests,
the worn-out soil… when we
discover we can't create any
thing. Our actions succeed as
well as putting sticky tape
over a chopped-off toe.

We change our posters, make
known that we're just one
piece in a puzzle with gazillions
of pieces. Two billion humans
no more noticeable than our sun
on a map of stars. In the vast
world food web, humans might
not even make the poster as a
speck. We stare at our reflection
and again ask, "What good is it?"
—and can we answer ourselves?

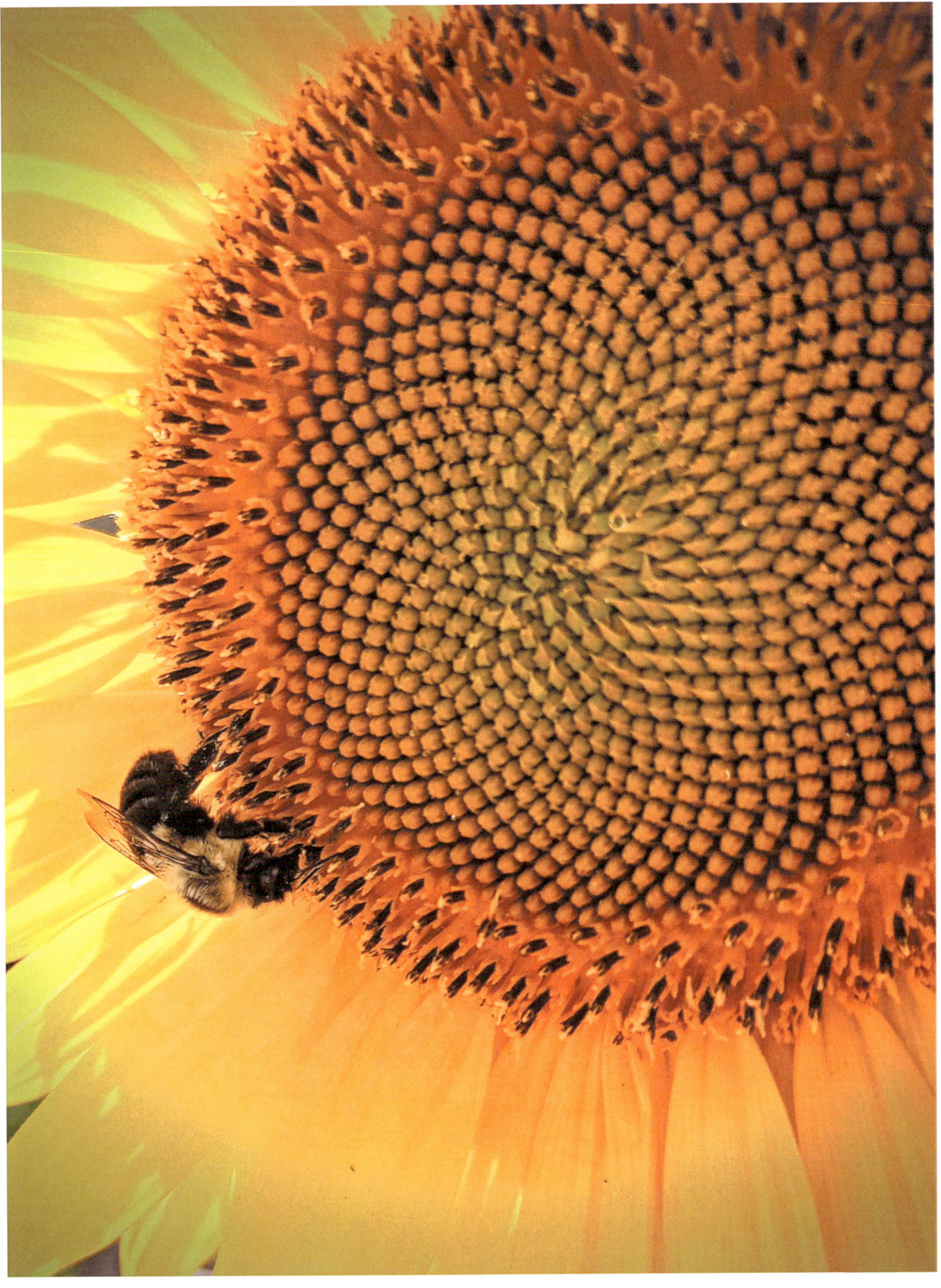

ROCK SKIPPING

Like flat stones
skipping across
flat water
just nicking
the surface
here and there
until sinking
soundlessly,
seemingly
causeless
ripples
diminishing

thoughts
hit, skip away,
too fast
to sink
into ideas
or action.

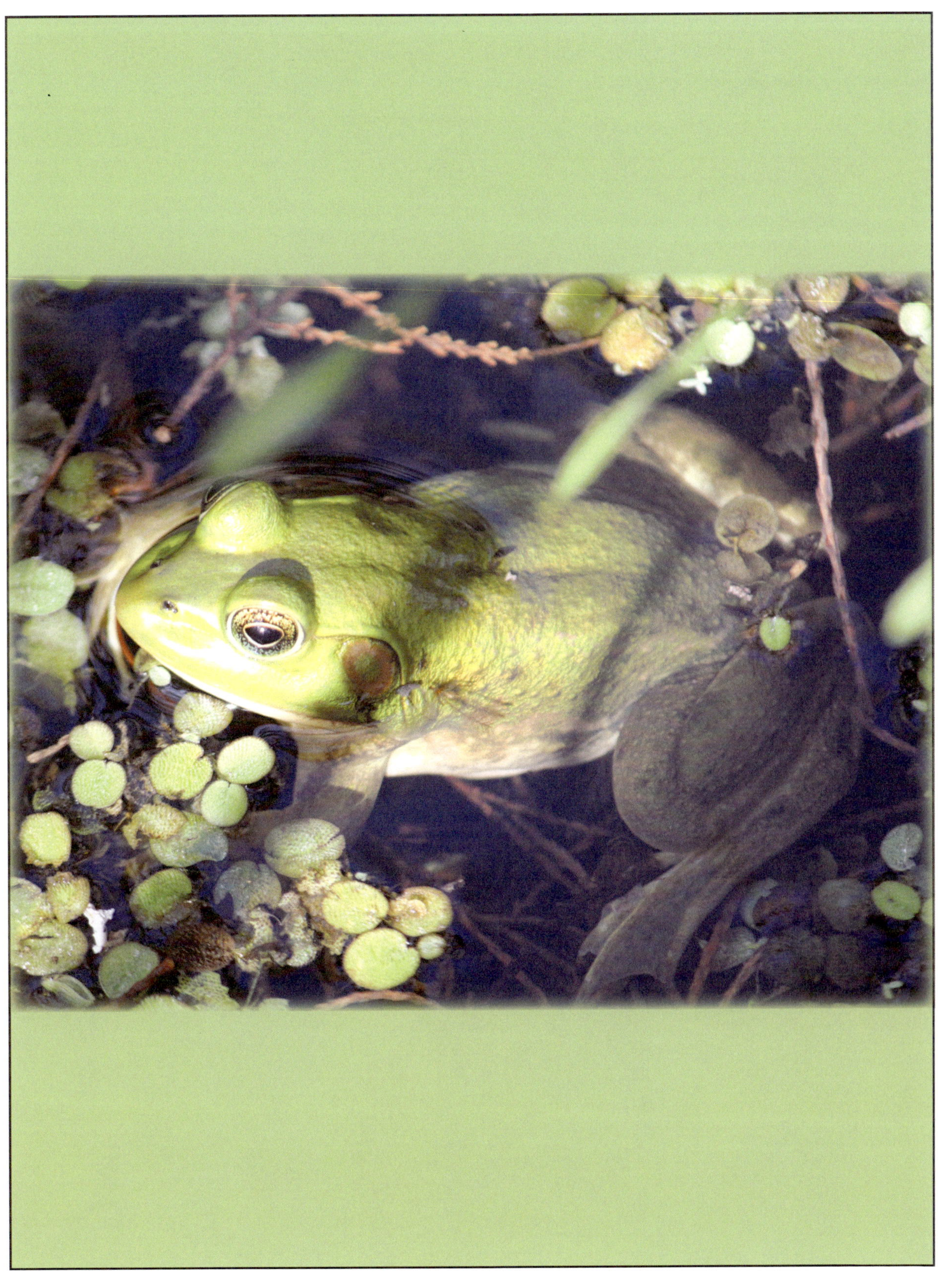

SERENITY

Light shivers and shakes awake misty air.

Water ripples, bubbles. Somewhere a splash.

Reeds sway, shake, then bend morning wind.

A snake winds water, sends whorls shoreward.

A bittern erupts ahead of a gator
emerging, nostrils first.

An osprey snatches a fish, flies it to the top
of a snag.

Tourists sigh. "So still." "So peaceful." They
turn backs to the scene and go for coffee.

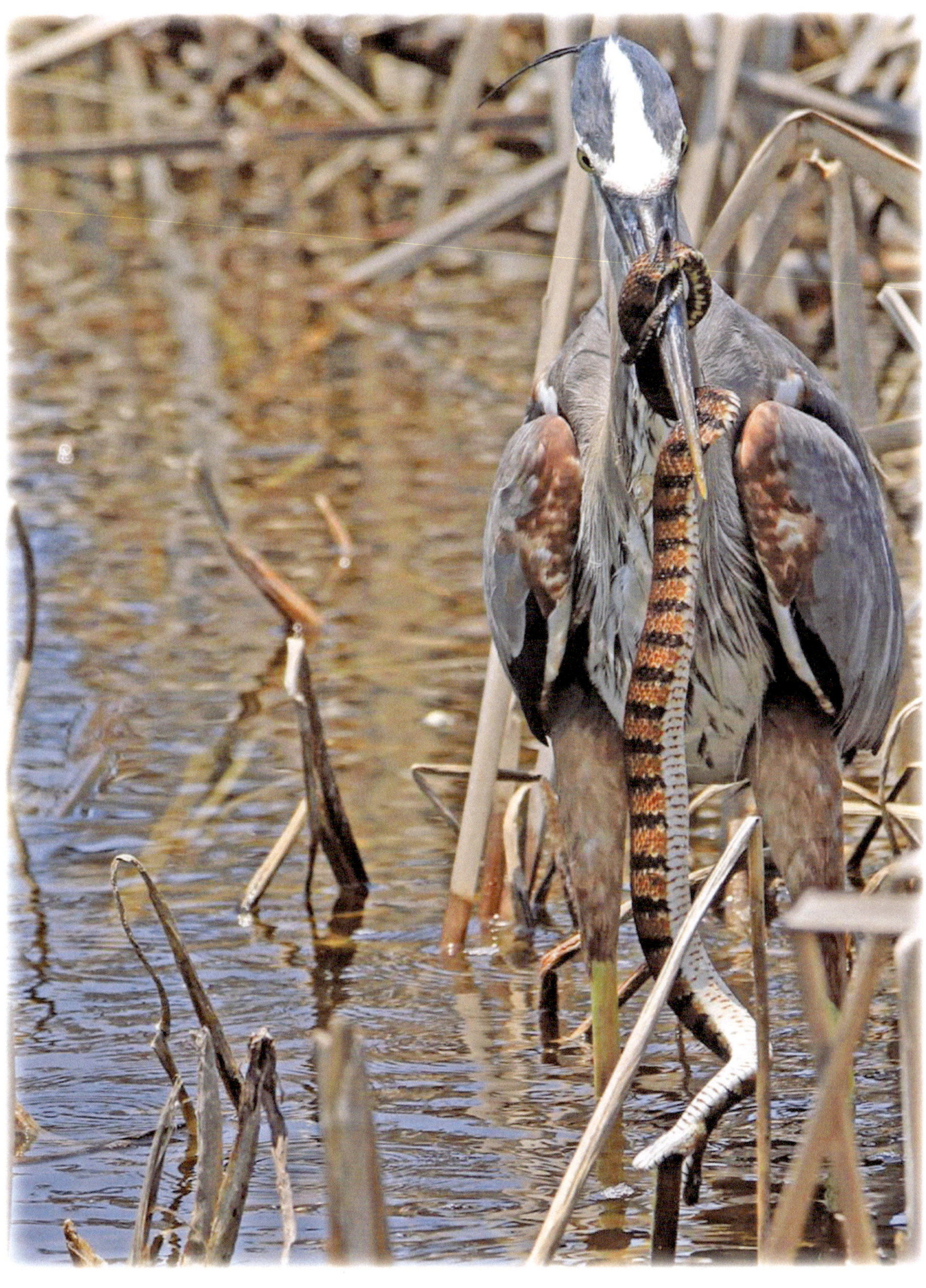

CONSIDERING

Consider nudibranchs
and cacti; butter
and dragons that fly;
a bird six feet tall
and another smaller
than your baby toe;
a cetacean a hundred
times your size;
bacteria thriving
on your eyes;
trees refreshing
our air; soil
purifying our water
sources; invisible
magnetic forces
protecting our Earth;
gravity holding
Earth's orbit firm.

Consider joyous, childlike
wonder for this banquet
daily set before us,
more than we
could plan, imagine
or make …

how can we ask for more?

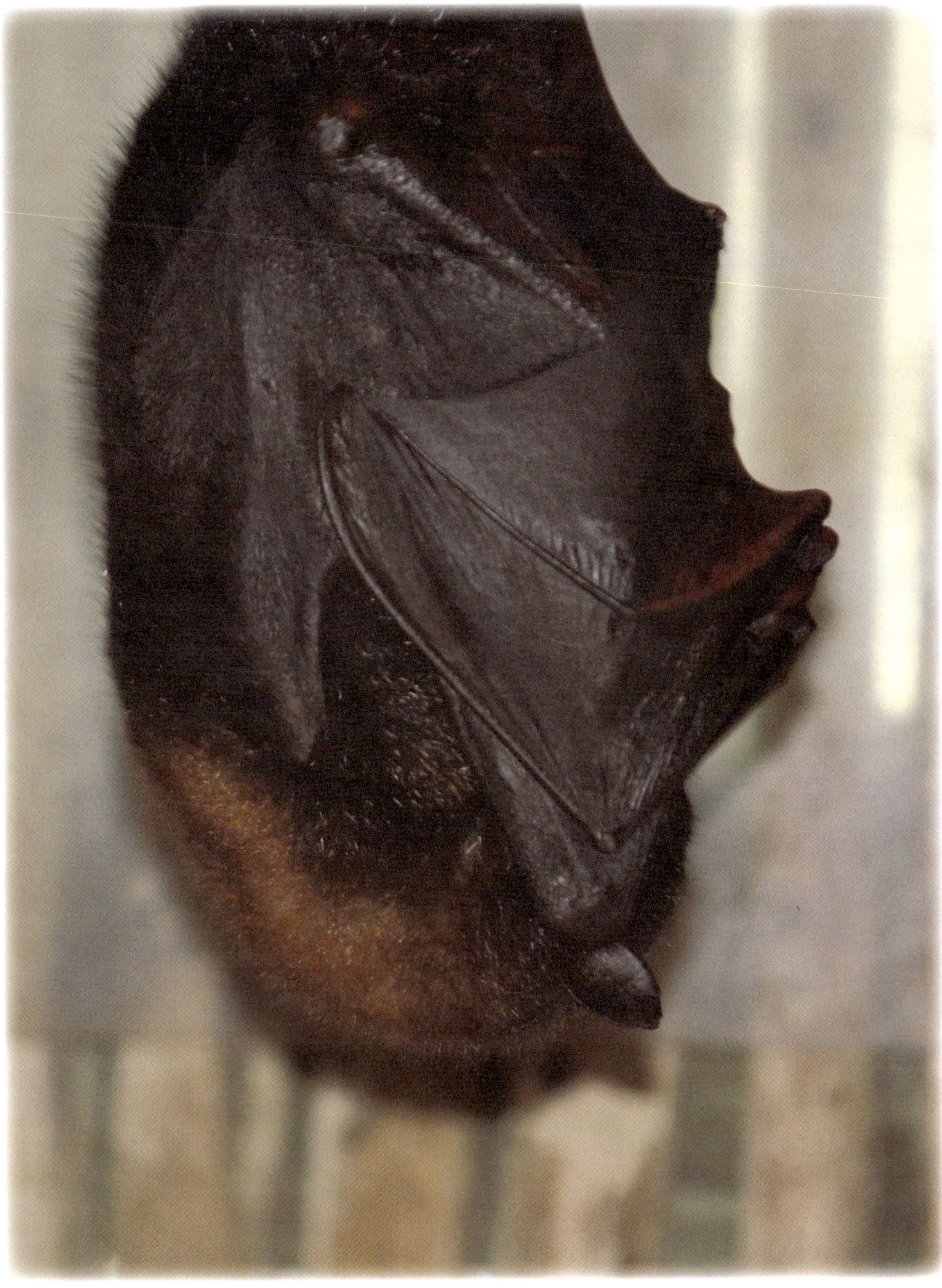

WHAT IF …

What if stronger, longer
storms are just a natural cycle,
not climate change at all?

What if hotter, larger
and more frequent wildfires
are coincidental only
to those stronger storms,
not climate change at all?

What if rising seas
drowning coastal towns
and islands are unrelated
to stronger storms or more
frequent wildfires and
not climate change at all?

What if more frequent,
longer droughts driving
thermometers to new heights
and dropping fresh water
reserves to thirsty levels
are isolated events, nothing
to do with stronger storms,
hotter wildfires, and drowning
cities, and not climate change,
no, not at all?

What if dying pollinators,
decimated bird, amphibian
reptilian, and fish populations,
along with dying coral reefs
and forests, are unconnected
to burning and bulldozed
habitat, dirty air, clogged
waterways, rising temperatures
and seas, and seasonal shifts
with longer, stronger storms …
unconnected and not part
of climate change at all?

What if increasing pandemics,
increased lung and heart
issues, heat stroke, famines,
and shorter life spans
are somehow isolated
from floods, polluted water,
filthy air, rising temperatures,
decreasing food supplies, and any
other of the etcetera lumped
into the name of climate change
but aren't climate change at all?

What if dirty air, polluted
water, and worsening weather
and health can't be stopped
or slowed by using one less
plastic straw, by eating one less
hamburger, by driving one day
less, by picking up one plastic bag
off the beach, or by using
only what you need? —
but what if they can?

What if caring can save us …
          but no one does … ?

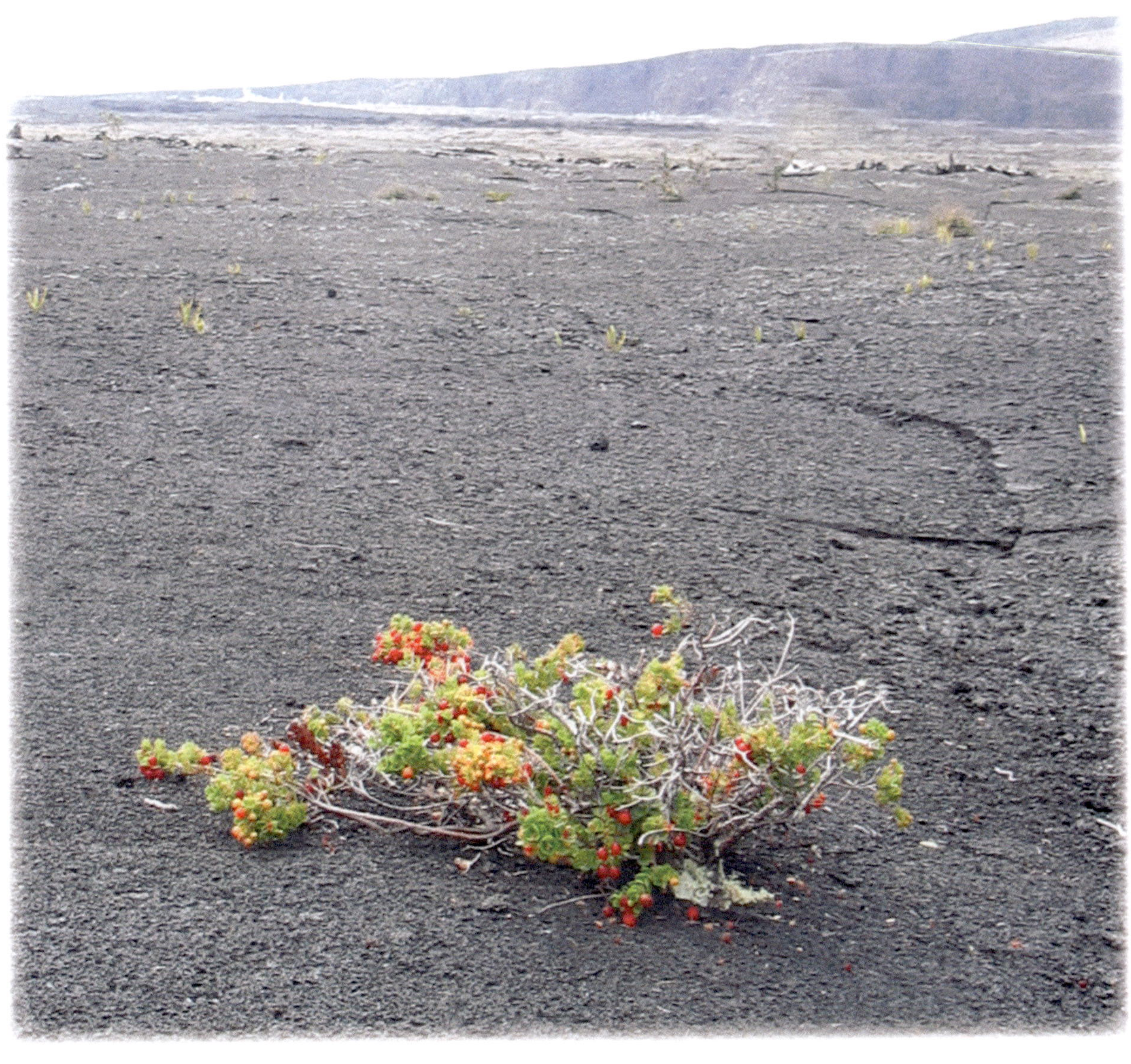

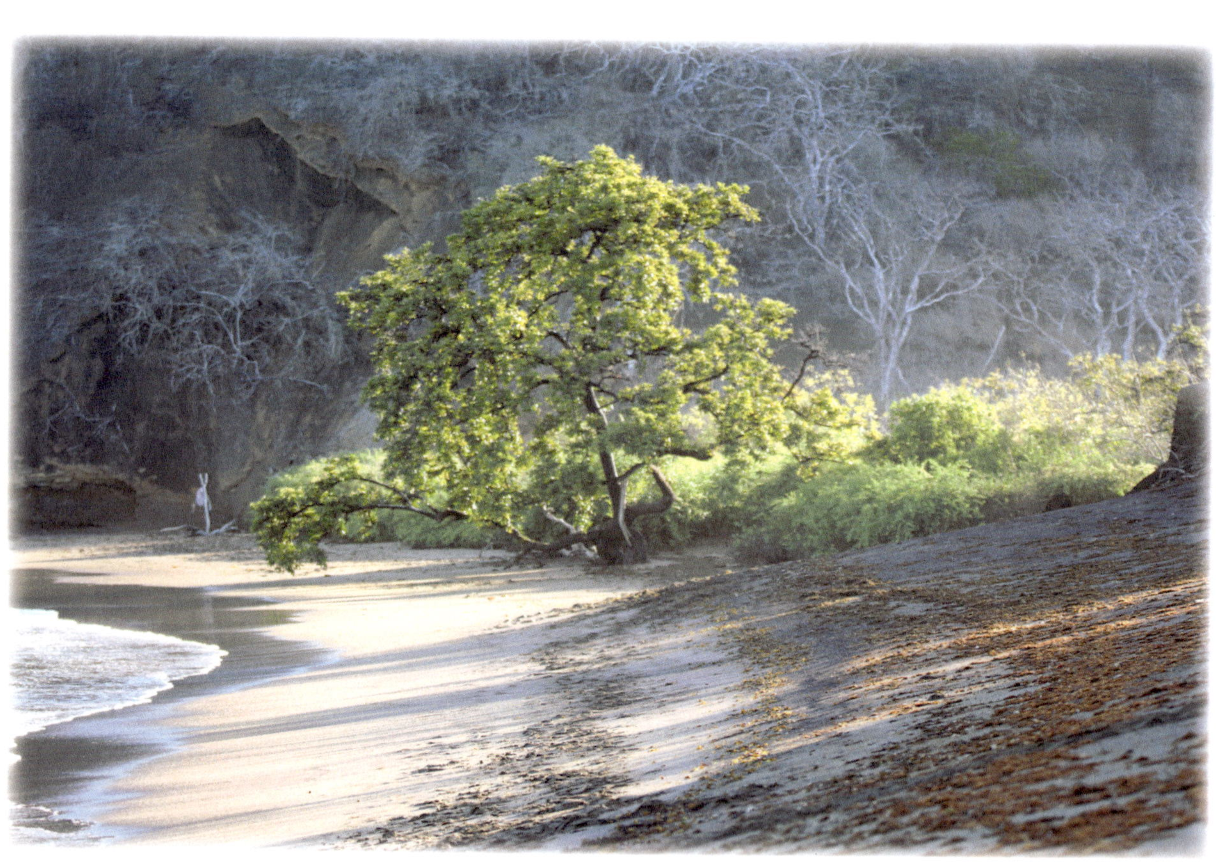

HEALING

"Those who contemplate the beauty of the earth find reserves of strength that will endure as long as life lasts. There is something infinitely healing in the repeated refrains of nature—the assurance that dawn comes after night, and spring after winter."

—Rachel Carson, catalyst for the modern environmental movement
and author of *Silent Spring*

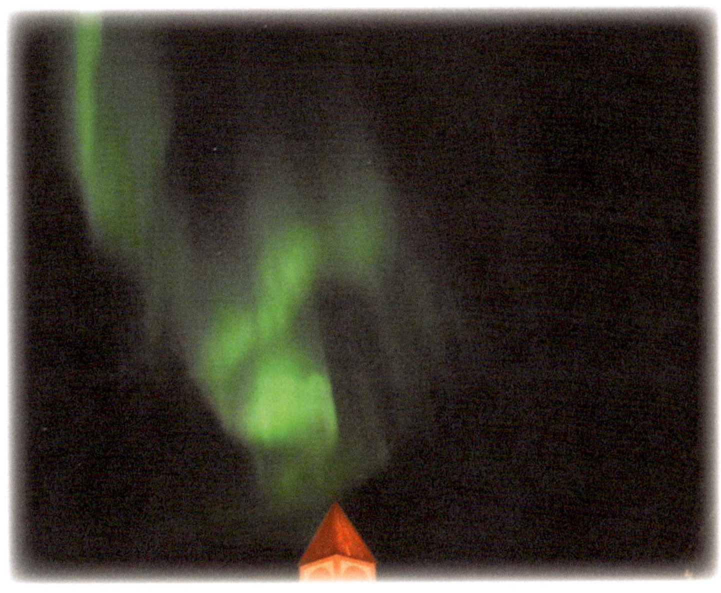

PURPLE POOP

Purple bird poop upon the skylight
proclaims blackberry season and fall
diminishing light. Longer shadows
stretch north luring blackberry eating
birds who take flight for winter lands
where berries flourish all year.

Goldfinches fade. Western tanagers
spark like a late sunset, then vanish.
Hummingbirds pause at flowers
where petals droop and fall. Some
birds linger for the last few drops
of sweet summer before beginning
their autumnal journey even while
blackberry memories perfume fall air.

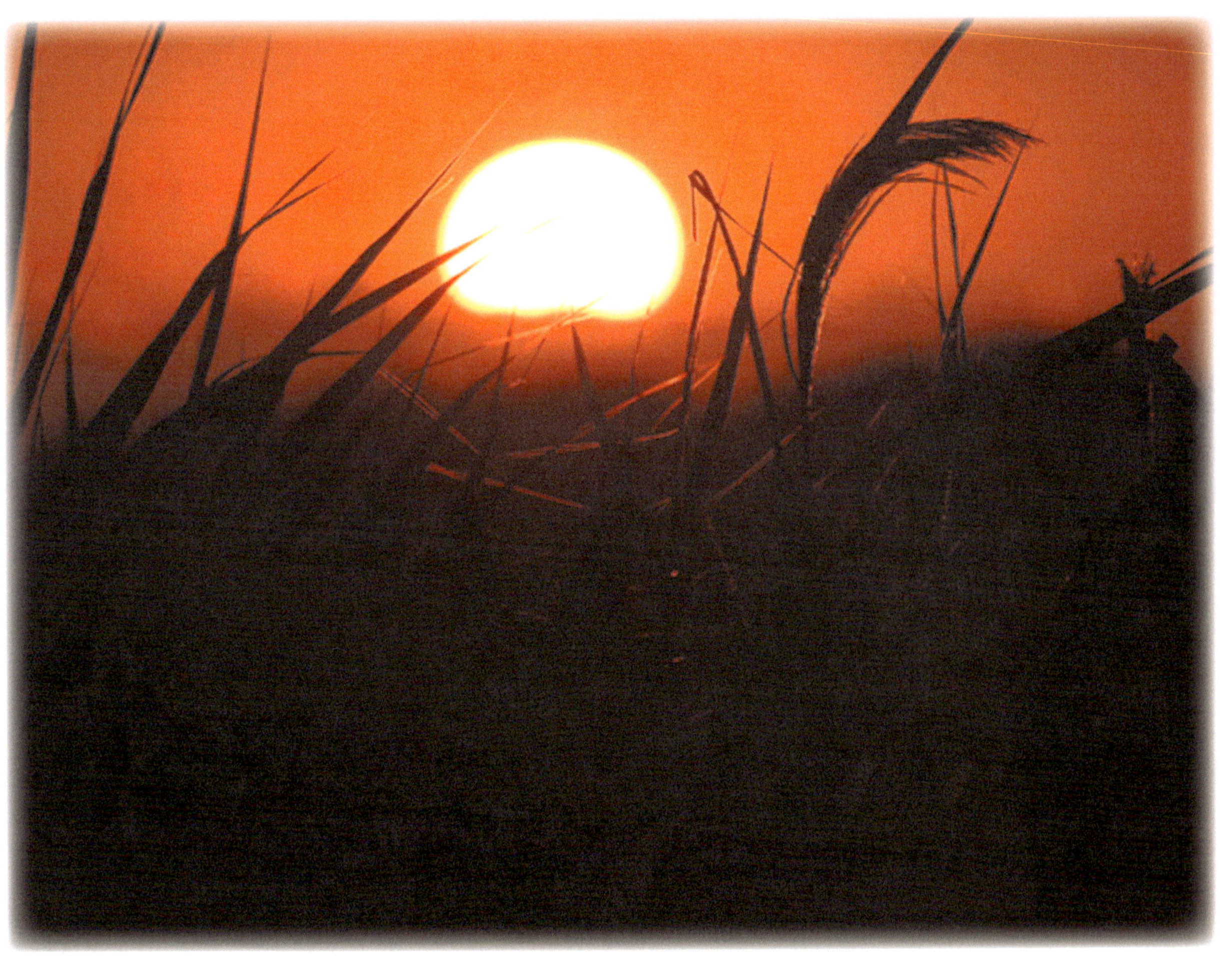

SULA NEBOUXII
(BLUE-FOOTED BOOBY)

Show me your feet
of vivid blue,
and I'll fall madly
in love with you.
I'll bob my head
and spread my wings,
then I, too, will lift
my feet of blue.
Whistle to me …
… I'll quack to you.
Oh! come to me
and be my love!
We can raise a chick
or two with booby
feet of vivid blue.

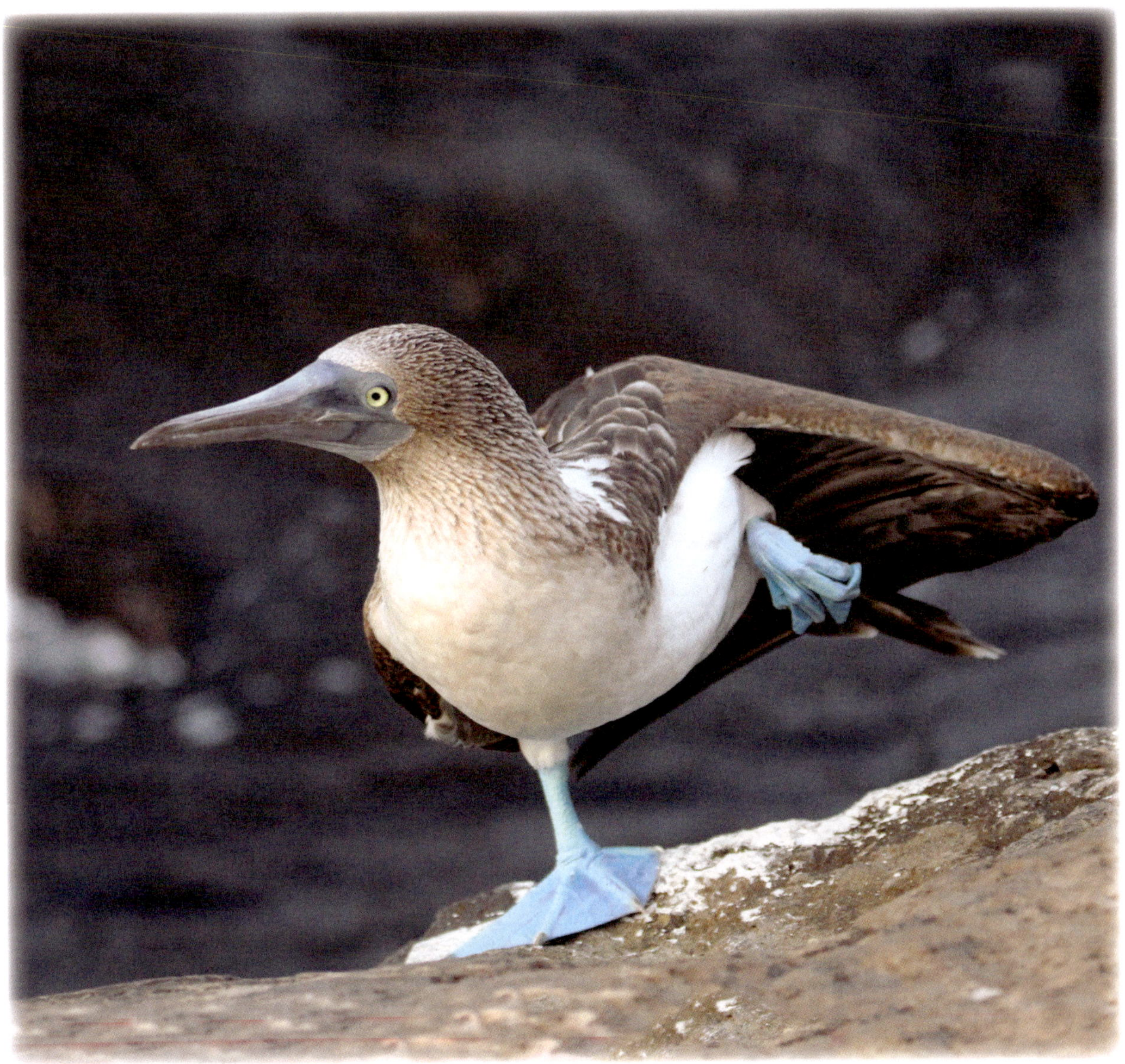

REFLECTED GLORY

Across still water, a pelican's wings
dip toward another pelican, tips almost
touching like thoughts between
passing strangers making brief
eye contact. A breeze erases
the pelican below and the other,
alone, rises to search the sky

where fire red, gold, pink, purple,
yellow flicker as clouds dance
with wind, twirl colors like ribbons.

Sun slips away, taking reflected
glory, leaving clouds, grey and white
and alone hanging in a darkening sky
leaving a moment of reflected glory
permanently etched in grateful memory.

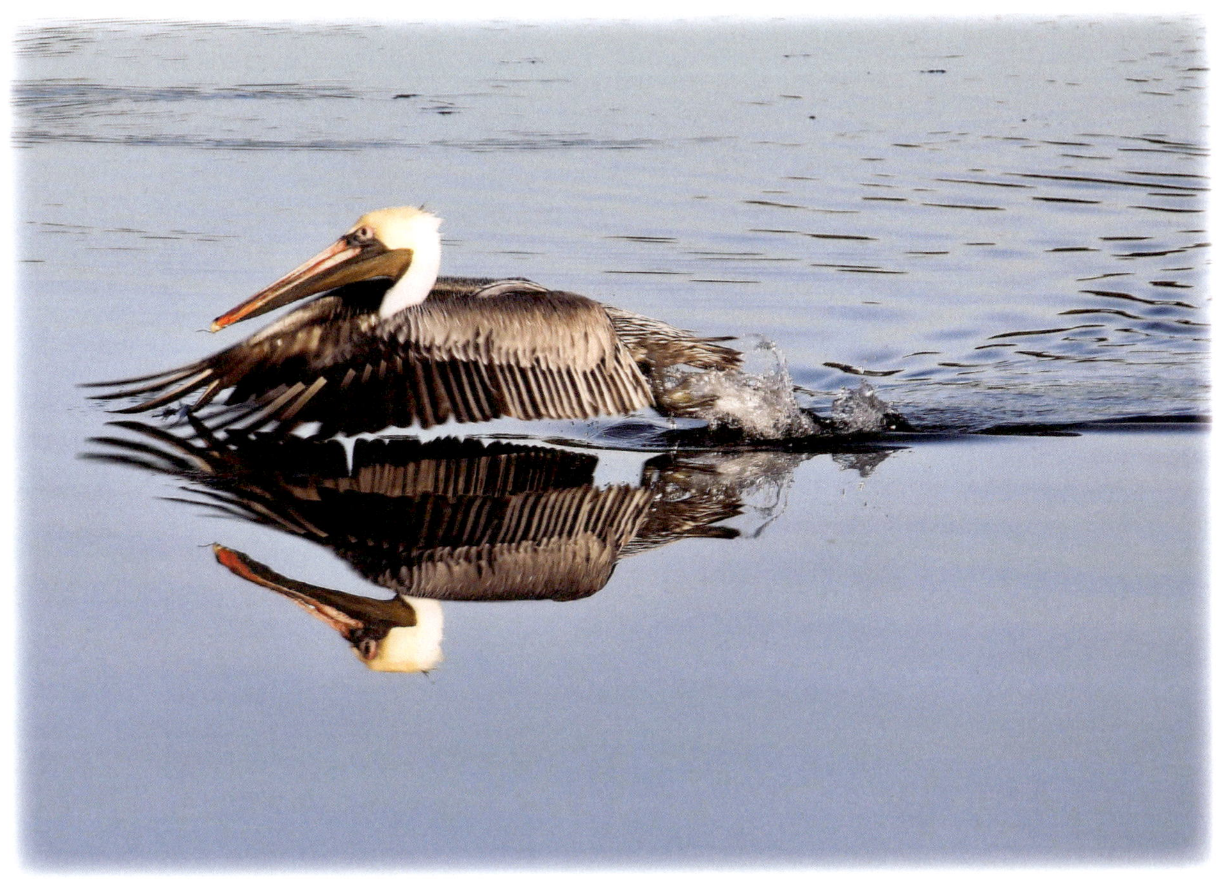

Butterflies & Chaos

Even the name sounds soft,
delicate, whimsical. Origin
of the name is as unclear
as butterfly evolution.

Weighing less than a gram,
vulnerable to irritable winds,
    droughts,
    loss of flowers,
    hungry birds
yet somehow
            for 100 million years
a survivor who enthralls humans,
sculpts imagination with magic.

From ungainly, even bizarre
caterpillar to flitting color
dancing among flowers,
each promises transformation
as reality and renewal
for soul and spirit,
our psyche on the wing.

Butterflies drink crocodile tears,
steal milk and butter,
and live in a nervous stomach.
They symbolize chaos theory,
with a wing flutter in China
birthing a Caribbean hurricane
while brightening our dreams.

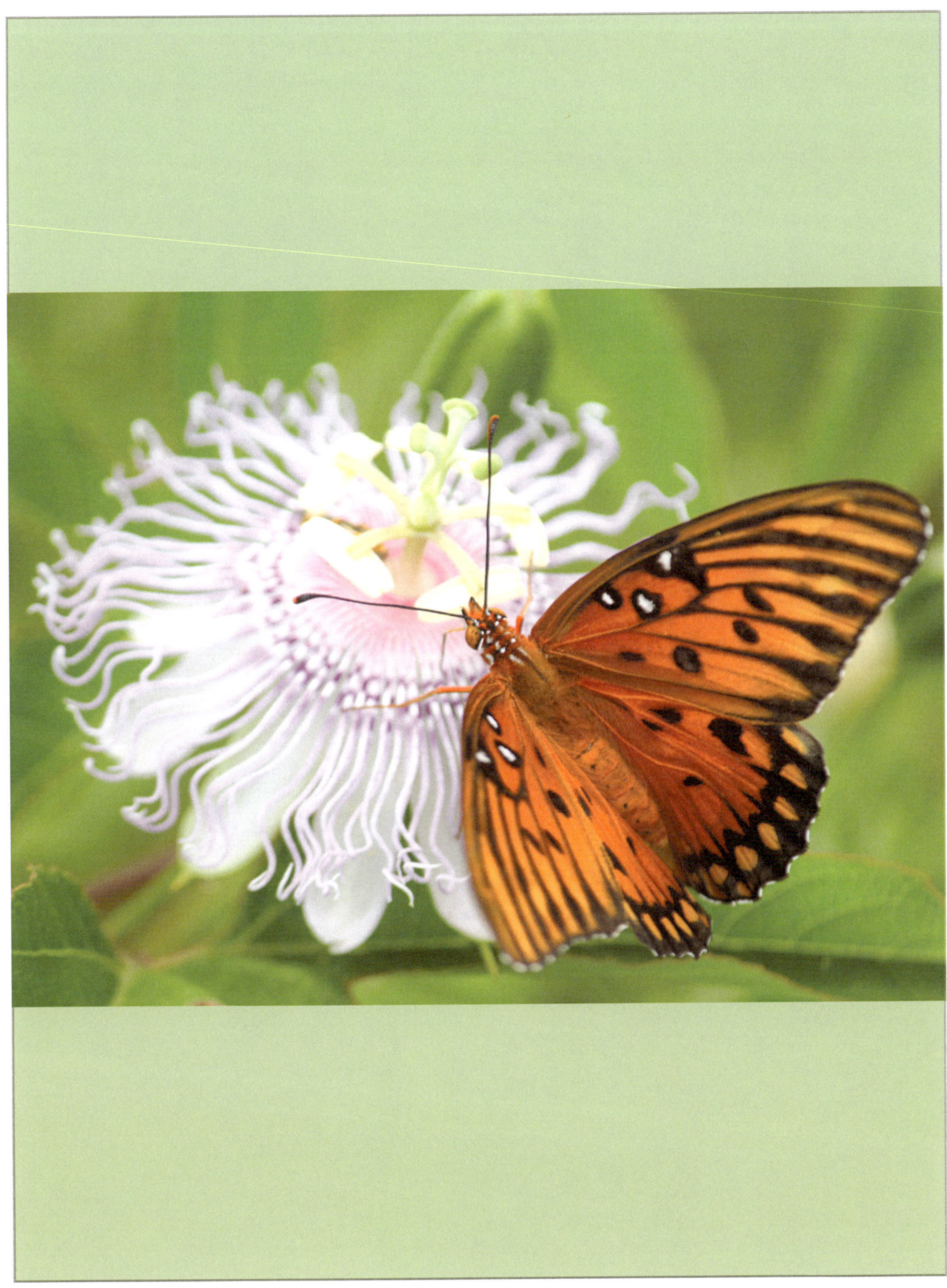

SEASONAL SYNESTHESIA

Clapping blue sky and brisk yellow sun
contradict the golden big leaf maple
leaves spinning off pegs, joining purple
cousins dancing across brilliant, almost-
neon, spring green hayfields and lawns.

Adjacent hills alternate greens, deeply
dark Douglas fir whisper-touching lighter
cedars who carpet the forest floor
with older, rusted, scaly branchlets.

Splashes of color–maple, alder,
cascara–add texture to what,
in summer, appears as a wall of green.

Memories of spring rise, and I almost
forget that darker days push against
already-white Olympic peaks, scatter
…then gather into winter sky-river.

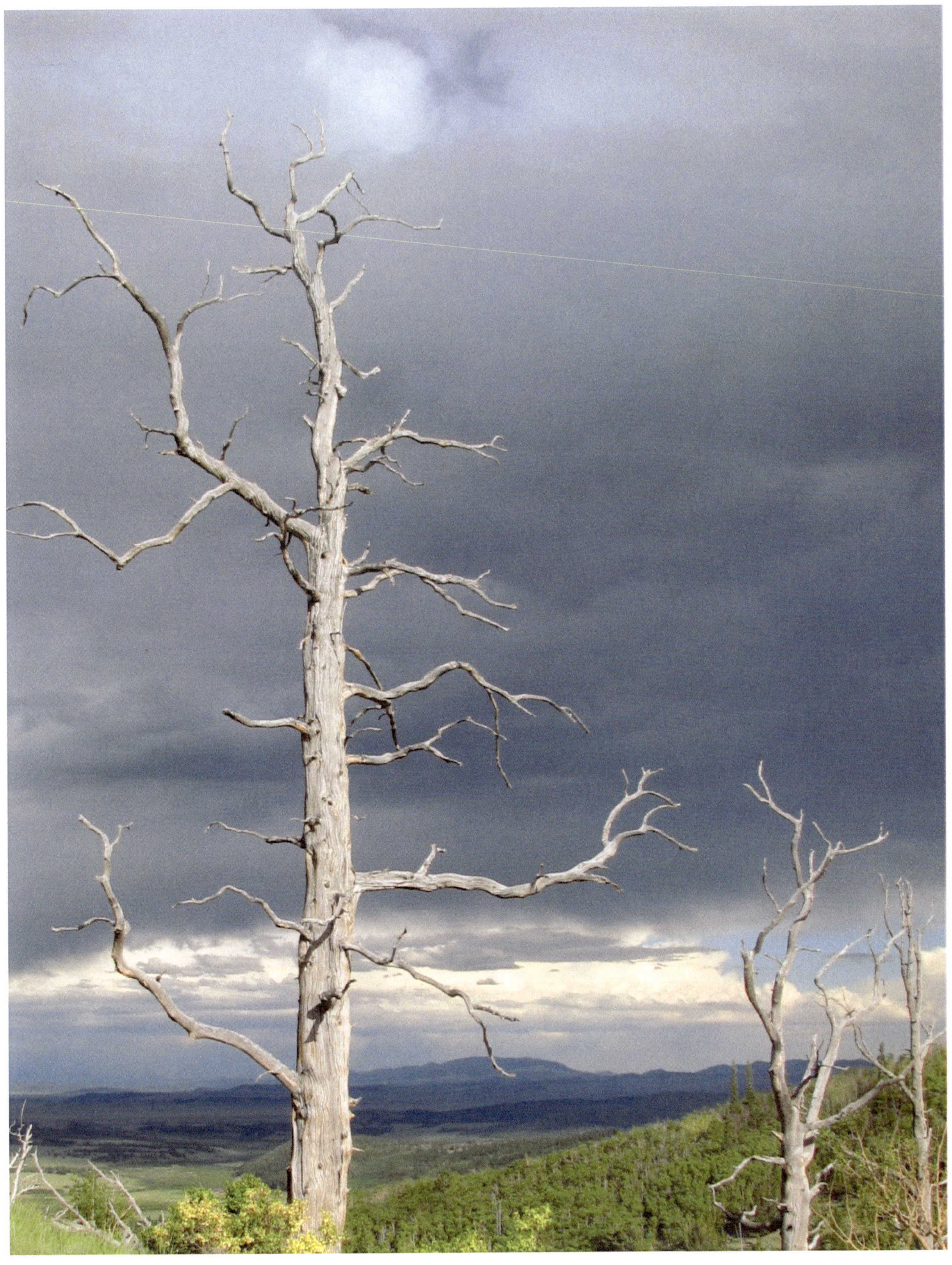

TENSION SPRING

A highly stressed spring
loses elasticity

    Spring slinking
    stretching and/or shrinking
        between one step and another
        between winter and summer
         between expectation and depression
        between plant budding and freezing

creating uncertain pitch
flowing or frozen
between warmth and chill
  wind and breeze
  yes and no
  to Hooke's law[*].

Restoring force is lost.

Call it climate change.
Call it climate stress.
Call it elastosis.
Call it fugue.

Loss of force and deflection,
gain of inability

to account for dawn
  grey
    chilly
      damp.

[*] Hooke's Law states that the extension of a spring is proportional to the load that is applied

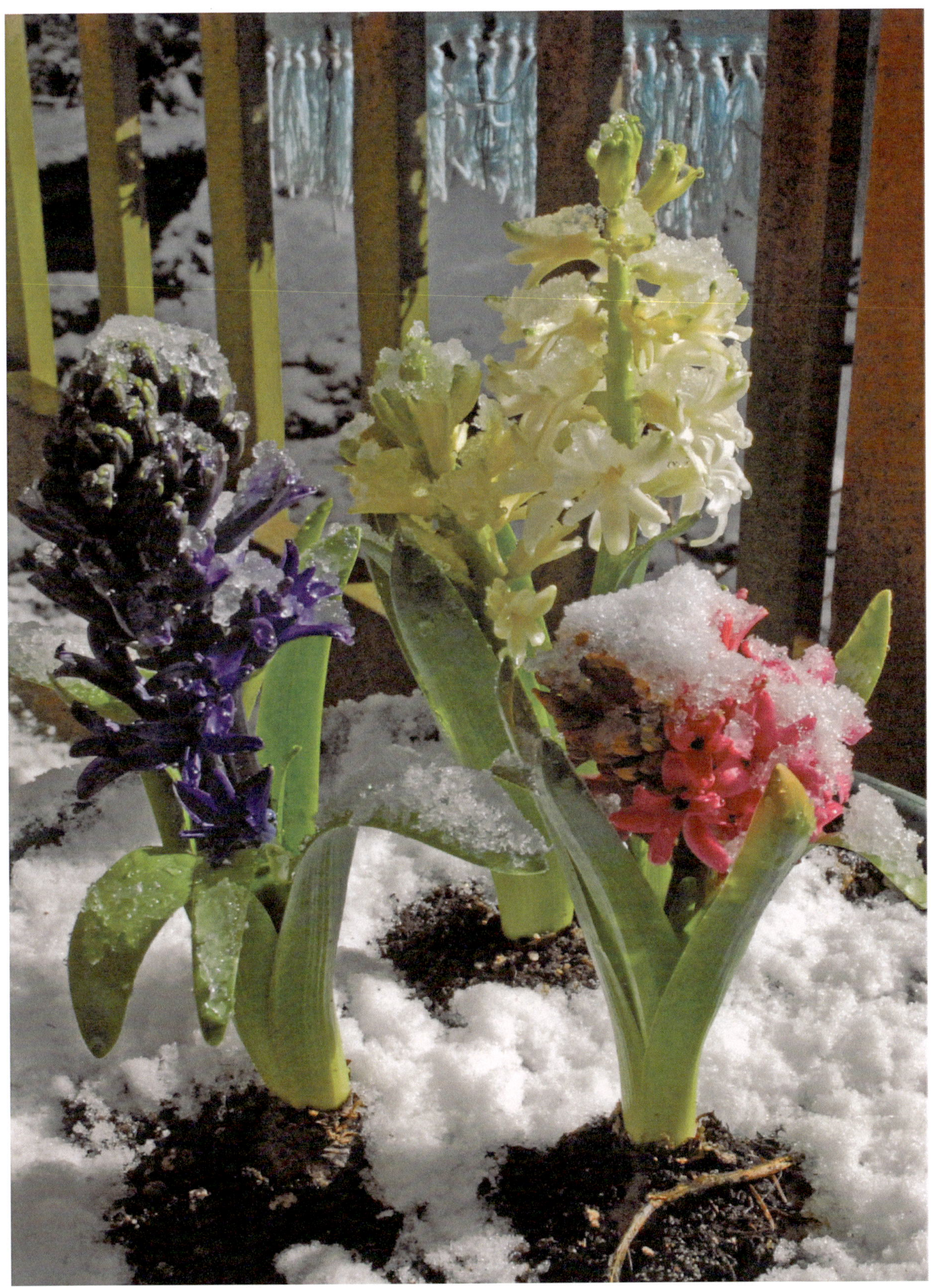

Fall

The water year has begun.
Rainforest is having a clear out.
Gales scrub branchlets and leaves
from trees worn out by spring
enthusiasm, summer drought,
and sudden temperature drops.
Debris swirl, branches and trees
snap, self-thinning and trimming.

Atmospheric rivers succumb
to gravitational embrace
and horizontal rain scours
trunks, rocks, and green needles
until each becomes a light-
reflecting mini-rainbows.
Fresh scent and brilliance belie
dark clouds and earlier sunsets.

Creeks, roads, and sidewalks
channel rivers where wandering
salmon swim upstream until
cascading into a more
familiar streambed. Birds
and squirrels flock to feeders.
Crows catch air currents,
join them to swoop and dive,
our winter's arch angels who
celebrate the return of the fall.

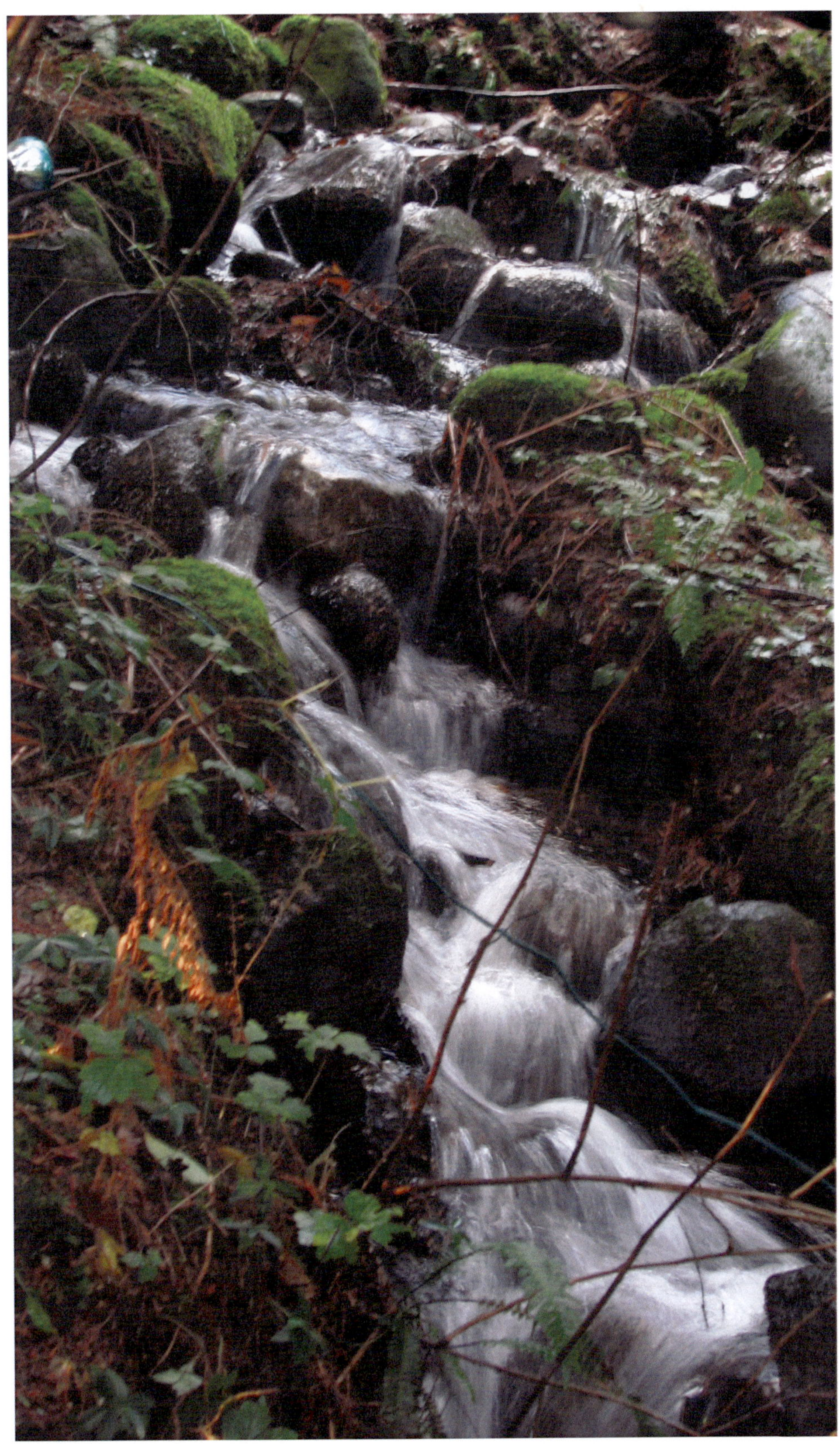

                                                 Marian Blue and Cherie Ude-Crowe

ECLIPSE

Oh brave and worthy moon,
small, alone, you cut between
Earth and gigantic Sun,
blotting out starlight,
absorbing white, hot heat,
sweeping dust like ash
into ancient craters.

Calliope hummingbird*,
smallest North American
avian, dives across
gigantic** goshawk path,
shimmering hummer color
diverting goshawk flight
from the secreted nest
beneath a rhododendron leaf.

* A calliope hummingbird weighs about 1/10 of an ounce
** A goshawk can weigh 2-3 pounds

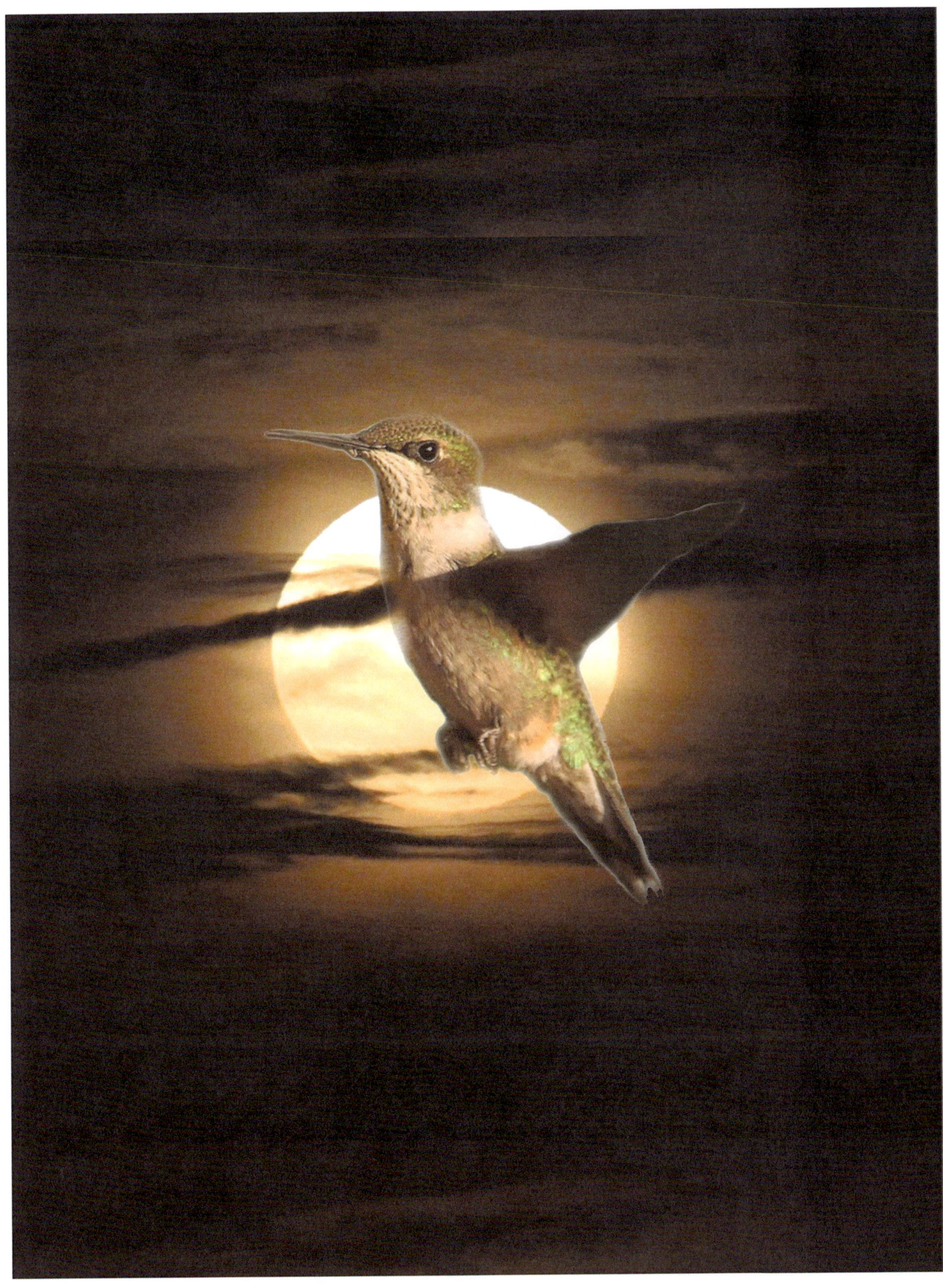

BEGATS OF GRATITUDE

Do squirrels intend cuteness
as a thank you, holding
my given peanut between
their two front, four-toed paws
as if praying? Does gratitude
sculpt their behavior?

Do birds know their singing
brightens my mind, lightens
thoughts into expectations
of a harmonious day? Does
gratitude shape their sound?

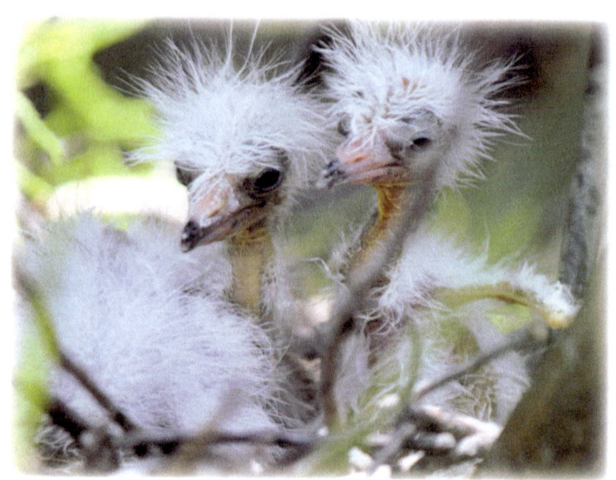

Does snow understand silence
as bestowal of peace and grace,
unique flakes freestyle dancing
around new shapes growing
through the night? Does
gratitude quilt the snow
into this downy comforter?

Does water choose liquid form
to transform cool drinks to sighs,
wash away sweaty work,
create surf, river and rain sounds
to relieve stress and boost
well-being? Does gratitude
create this watery state?

A world new every day
yet the same, transforming
ordinary moments
and habitual actions
into our daily blessings,
into gifts of gratitude.

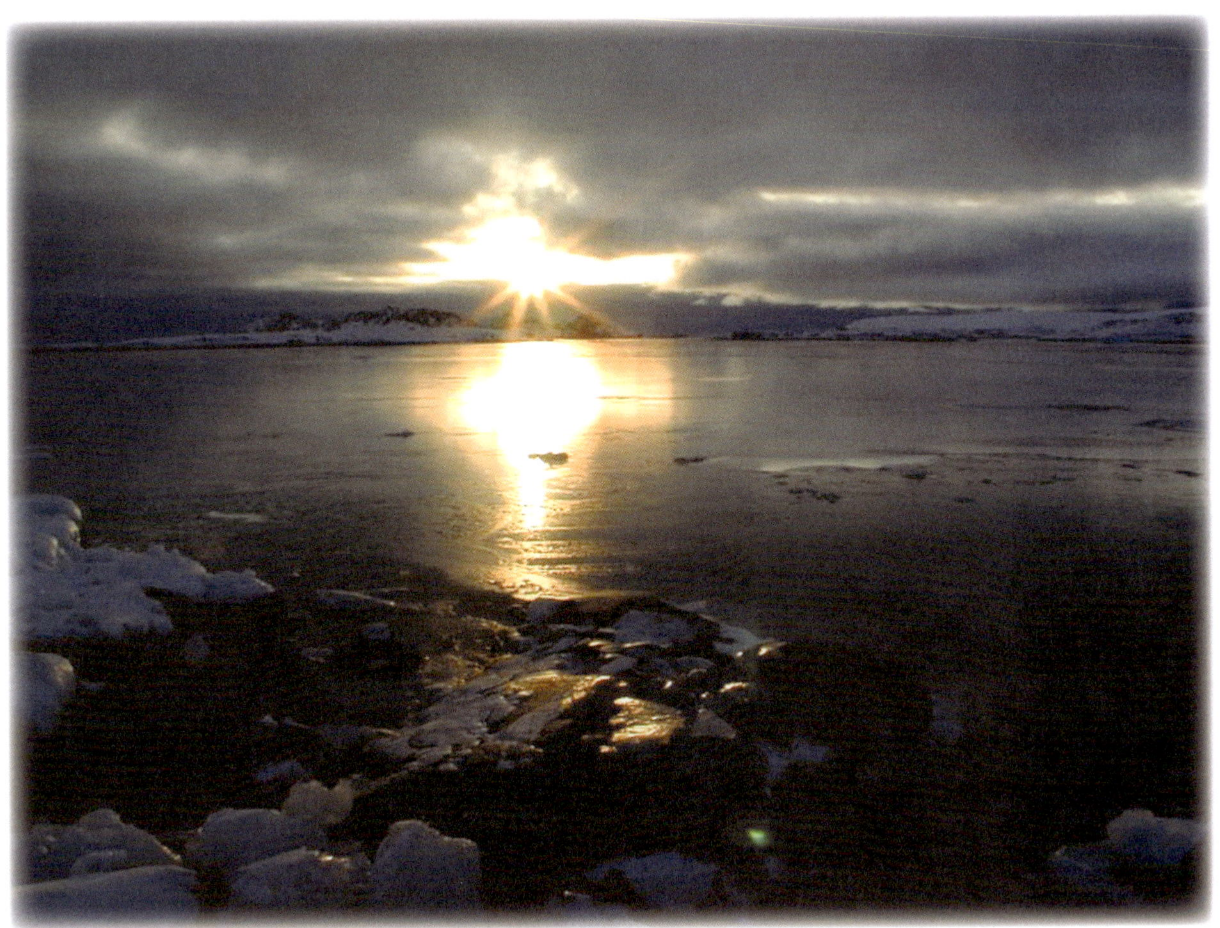

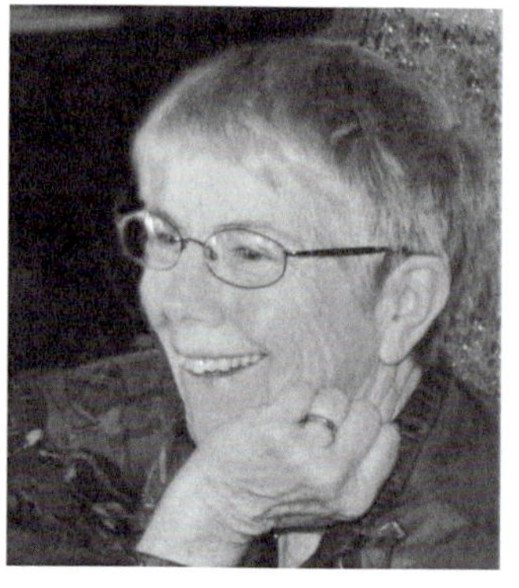

Marian Blue

Blue has lived in climates ranging from the dramatic chill within the shadow of Mt. Sopris, Colorado to the sunny warmth of the Dominican Republic in the Caribbean. She currently lives in the woods of Whidbey Island in the mossy and dark shadows of the northwest. In every environment, she's found ways to interact with different species, playing host to deer, crows, wolves, and other wildlife as well as her own rescue/foster dogs, parrots, goats, ducks, and more. She's always been grateful she had the opportunity to take the Basic Wildlife Rehabilitation skills seminar and receive extensive training through both Sound Water Stewards of Island County (formerly Beach Watchers) and Marine Mammal Stranding Network. She also attended the Forest Stewardship Program, Washington State Department of Natural Resources through Washington State University. She is a proud member of ILCW (International League of Conservation Writers).

Blue began writing as a journalist in the 1970s and went on to publish and edit essays, fiction, and poetry in various magazines and books. She taught writing and literature in various locations, the most recent at Skagit Valley College, before retiring in 2016 and celebrating with a trip to the Galápagos Islands. More about her writing and books appears on the Sunbreak Press Web page, where you can also read her Conservation blog.

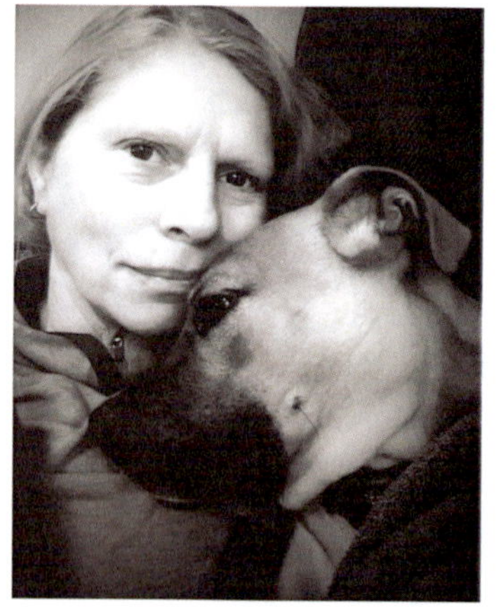

Cherie Ude-Crowe

Ude-Crowe has spent a lifetime with camera in hand as she has traveled. Many of her photos reflect Earth's beauty and drama in places as diverse as Antarctica and Australia. She has also captured landscapes and the creatures who live there through North and South America, the Caribbean, and Europe. She has professionally designed Web pages for special events — such as weddings, festivals, and reunions — and photographed weddings, baby showers, and reunions.

Ude-Crowe's work has appeared in books and magazines, including cover art, as well as on Web sites. See her images and learn more about her at Cherie Ude Photography on Facebook. She currently lives in New York on Long Island with her husband, John Crowe, and her gorgeous dogs, Drummer and Charlie.

For more about Ude-Crowe, visit her LinkedIn site.

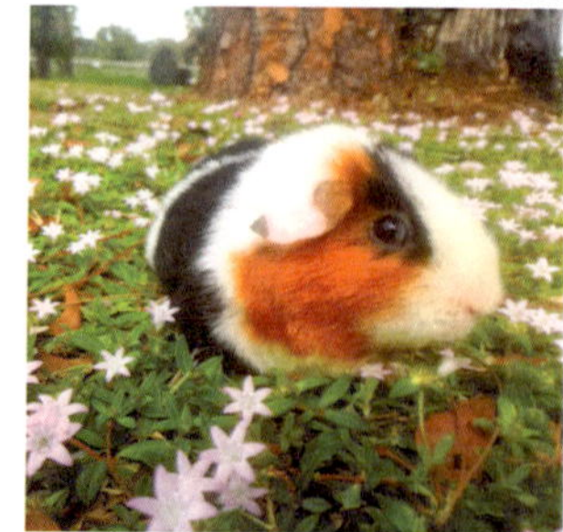

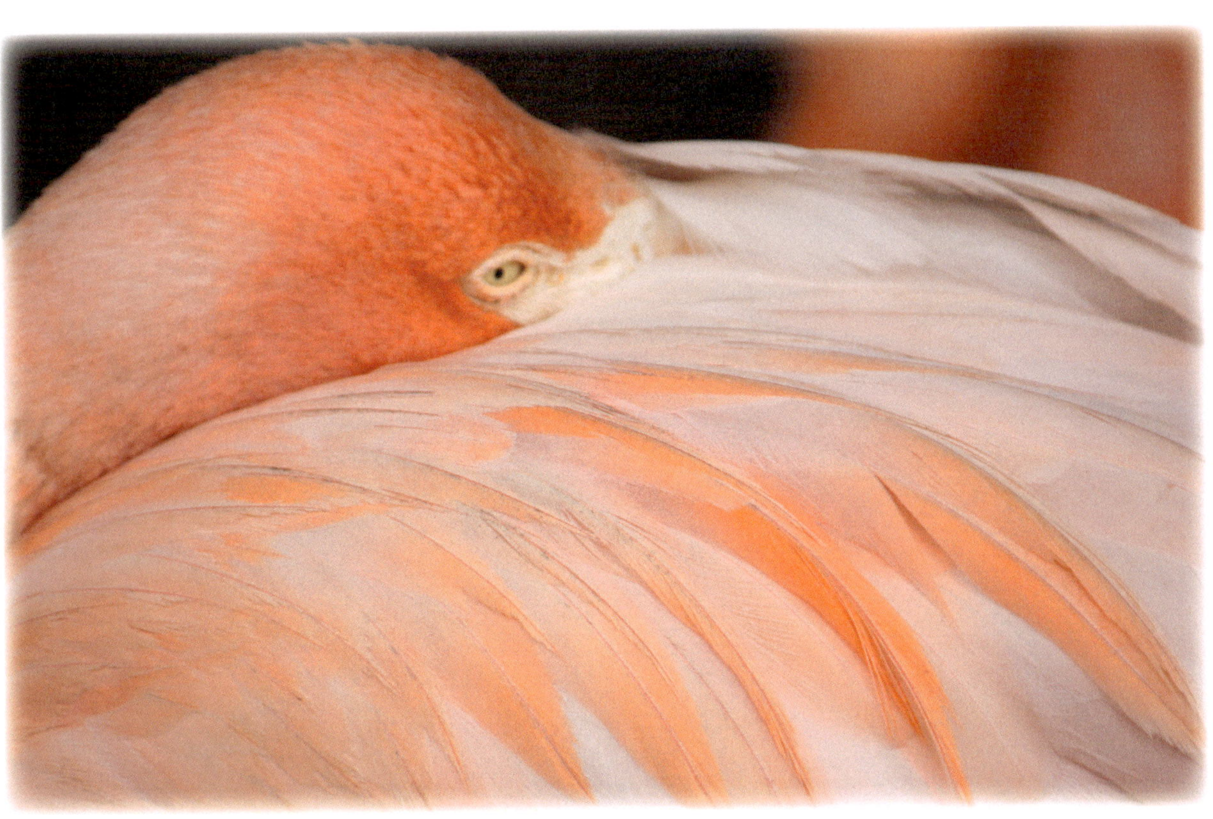

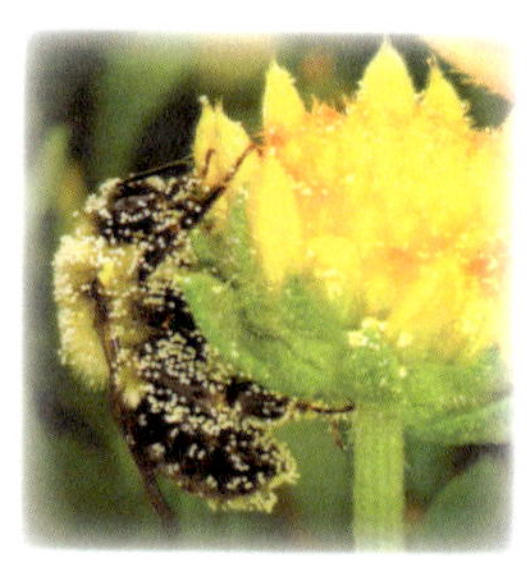

OTHER BOOKS

SAILING OFF THE HOOK
A Collection of short stories

QUANTUM CONSEQUENCES
Novel

INTERPRETATIVE GUIDE TO WESTERN NORTHWEST WEATHER FORECASTS
Humorous Nonfiction – Photos by many

MUSIC TO MY YEARS, LIFE AND LOVE BETWEEN THE NOTES
As told by Artie Kane to Marian Blue & JoAnn Kane

SEA OF VOICES, ISLE OF STORY
Anthology of Short Stories, edited by Celeste Mergens & Marian Blue

HOW MANY WORDS FOR RAIN
Poetry by Marian Blue and Photographs by Lynne Hann on Rain

THE 1993-1994 SOUTHEAST WRITER'S HANDBOOK: THE BEAUTY AND BUSINESS OF WRITING FOR AND BY SOUTHEASTERN WRITERS
Edited by Marian Blue

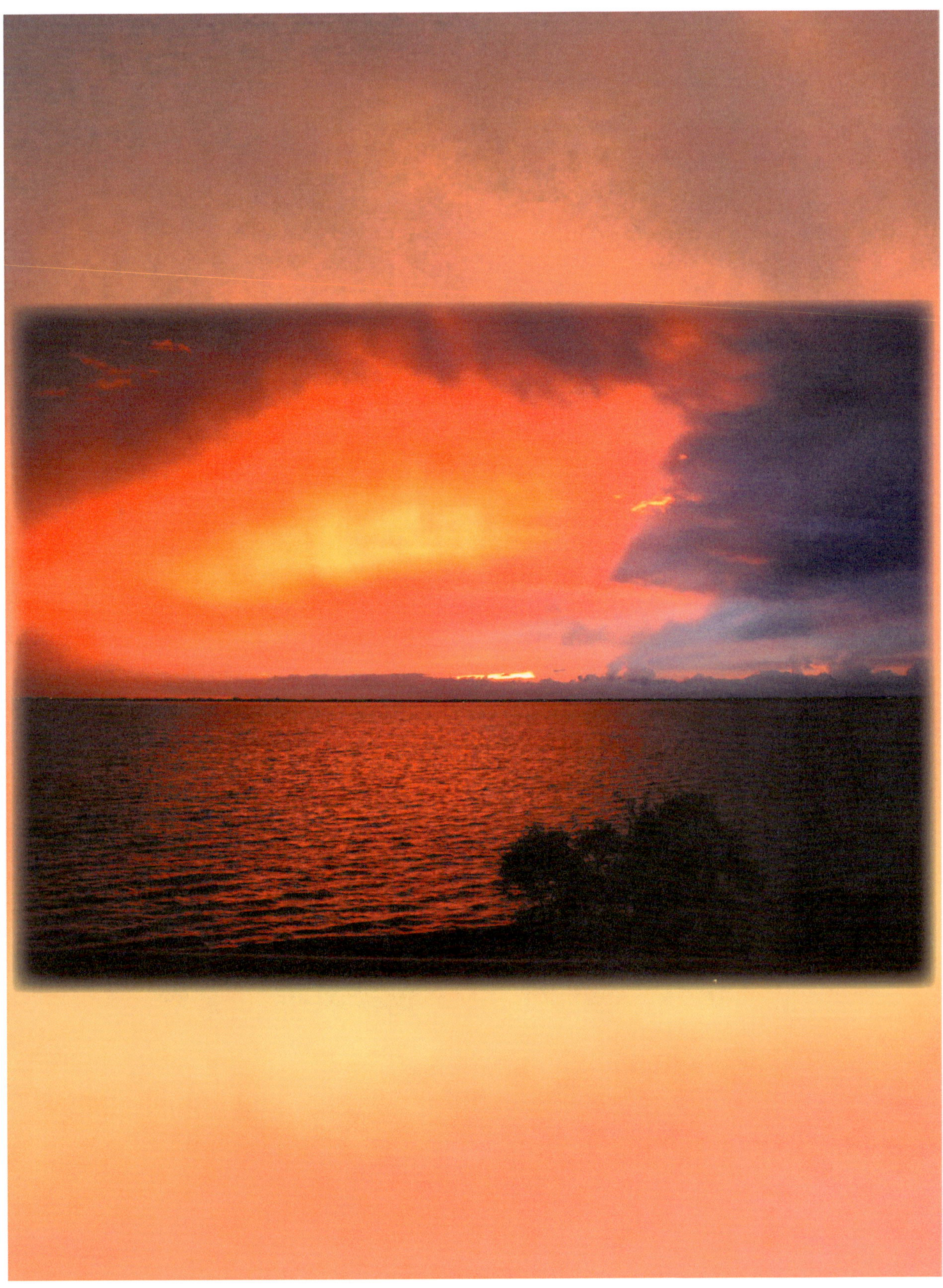